10° 11° 12° 13° 14°
47° 47°

CARNIC ALPS

2042 Stelvio Pass

CADORE

6182 Tonale Pass

7394 M. Neto

Adamello 11670

Val Giudicaria

Caporetto

JULIAN ALPS

TRENTO

Val Sugana

Feltre

Belluno

Vittorio Veneto

Udine

Bainsizza Plateau

46

Val Camonica

Val Lagarina

R. Brenta

Riva

Tiarno

Rovereto

Asiago

M. Grappa 5780

Conegliano

Pordenone

Palma-nova

R. Isonzo

Gorizia

CARSO

Lago d'Idro

L. Garda

Altissimo 6844

M. Pasubio 7367

Thiene

Bassano

Cittadella

Lovadina

R. Piave

TRIESTE

Brescia

VERONA

Vicenza

R. Astico

Treviso

R. Tagliamento

Desenzano

Sirmione

Peschiera

PADUA

VENICE

Solferino

R. Mincio

R. Adige

MANTUA

45°

45°

R. Po

R. Po

Ferrara

A D R I A T I C   S E A

PARMA

BOLOGNA

RAVENNA

POLA

44°

44°

FLORENCE

PISA

ANCONA

43°

43°

11° 12° 13° 14°

WITH BRITISH GUNS IN ITALY

ITALIAN TROOPS CROSSING A SNOWFIELD IN THE TRENTINO

WITH BRITISH GUNS
IN ITALY

A TRIBUTE TO ITALIAN ACHIEVEMENT

HUGH DALTON

SOMETIME LIEUTENANT IN
THE ROYAL GARRISON ARTILLERY

The Naval & Military Press Ltd

published in association with

FIREPOWER
The Royal Artillery Museum
Woolwich

Published by
The Naval & Military Press Ltd
Unit 10 Ridgewood Industrial Park,
Uckfield, East Sussex,
TN22 5QE England
Tel: +44 (0) 1825 749494
Fax: +44 (0) 1825 765701
www.naval–military–press.com

in association with

FIREPOWER
The Royal Artillery Museum, Woolwich
www.firepower.org.uk

The Naval & Military
Press

MILITARY HISTORY AT YOUR
FINGERTIPS

… a unique and expanding series of reference works

Working in collaboration with the foremost
regiments and institutions, as well as acknowledged
experts in their field, N&MP have assembled a
formidable array of titles including technologically
advanced CD-ROMs and facsimile reprints of
impossible-to-find rarities.

*In reprinting in facsimile from the original, any imperfections are inevitably
reproduced and the quality may fall short of modern type and cartographic standards.*

TO
THE HIGH CAUSE
OF
ANGLO-ITALIAN FRIENDSHIP
AND UNDERSTANDING

" Nella primavera si combatte e si muore, o soldato."
M. PUCCINI, *Dal Carso al Piave.*

" So they gave their bodies to the commonwealth
and received, each for his own memory, praise
that will never die, and with it the grandest of all
sepulchres ; not that in which their mortal bones
are laid, but a home in the minds of men, where their
glory remains fresh to stir to speech or action as
the occasion comes by. For the whole earth is the
sepulchre of famous men ; and their story is not
graven only on stone over their native earth, but
lives on far away, without visible symbol, woven
into the stuff of other men's lives."
Funeral Speech of Pericles.

" Dying here is not death ; it is flying into the
dawn."   MEREDITH, *Vittoria.*

PREFACE

SO far as I know, no British soldier who served
on the Italian Front has yet published a book
about his experiences. Ten British Batteries
went to Italy in the spring of 1917 and passed through
memorable days. But their story has not yet been
told. Nor, except in the language of official
dispatches, has that of the British Divisions which
went to Italy six months later, some of which remained
and took part in the final and decisive phases of the
war against Austria. Something more should soon
be written concerning the doings of the British troops
in Italy, for they deserve to stand out clearly in the
history of the war.

This little book of mine is only an account, more or
less in the form of a Diary, of what one British soldier
saw and felt, who served for eighteen months on the
Italian Front as a Subaltern officer in a Siege Battery.
But it was my luck to see a good deal during that time.
Mine had been the first British Battery to come into
action and open fire on the Italian Front. And, as
my story will show, it was either the first or among

the first on most other important occasions, except in the Caporetto retreat, and then it was the last.

I have camouflaged the names of all persons mentioned throughout the book, except those of Cabinet Ministers, Generals and a few other notabilities.

For permission to reproduce photographs, I wish to thank the representatives in London of the Italian State Railways (12 Waterloo Place, S.W.), and my friend and brother officer, Mr Stuart Osborn.

H. D.

LONDON, *February* 1919

CONTENTS

PREFACE vii

PART I

INTRODUCTORY

CHAPTER I

THE ANGLO-ITALIAN TRADITION AND ITALY'S PART IN THE
WAR I

PART II

SOME EARLY IMPRESSIONS

CHAPTER II

FROM FOLKESTONE TO VENICE 10

CHAPTER III

FROM VENICE TO THE ISONZO FRONT 13

CHAPTER IV

THE WAR ON THE ISONZO FRONT 22

CHAPTER V

PALMANOVA 35

CHAPTER VI

AQUILEIA AND GRADO 40

CHAPTER VII

PAGE

A GRAMOPHONE AND A CHAPLAIN ON THE CARSO   .   .   43

CHAPTER VIII

A FRONT LINE RECONNAISSANCE   49

CHAPTER IX

AN EVENING AT GORIZIA   55

CHAPTER X

A CEMETERY AT VERSA   58

CHAPTER XI

UDINE   61

CHAPTER XII

THE BRITISH AND THE ITALIAN SOLDIER   64

CHAPTER XIII

I JOIN THE FIRST BRITISH BATTERY IN ITALY .   .   .   67

PART III

THE ITALIAN SUMMER OFFENSIVE, 1917

CHAPTER XIV

THE OFFENSIVE OPENS   72

CHAPTER XV

WE SWITCH OUR GUNS NORTHWARD   76

CONTENTS

CHAPTER XVI
THE FALL OF MONTE SANTO 79

CHAPTER XVII
THE CONQUEST OF THE BAINSIZZA PLATEAU . . . 84

CHAPTER XVIII
THE FIGHTING DIES DOWN 87

CHAPTER XIX
A LULL BETWEEN TWO STORMS 92

PART IV
THE ITALIAN RETREAT AND RECOVERY

CHAPTER XX
THE BEGINNING OF THE ENEMY OFFENSIVE . . . 97

CHAPTER XXI
FROM THE VIPPACCO TO SAN GIORGIO DI NOGARA . . 103

CHAPTER XXII
FROM SAN GIORGIO TO THE TAGLIAMENTO . . . 115

CHAPTER XXIII
FROM THE TAGLIAMENTO TO TREVISO 129

CHAPTER XXIV
THOUGHTS AFTER THE DISASTER 134

CHAPTER XXV

FERRARA, ARQUATA AND THE CORNICE ROAD . . . 144

PAGE

CHAPTER XXVI

REFITTING AT FERRARA 151

PART V

A YEAR OF RESISTANCE AND OF PREPARATION

CHAPTER XXVII

IN STRATEGIC RESERVE 162

CHAPTER XXVIII

THE FIRST BRITISH BATTERY UP THE MOUNTAINS . . 169

CHAPTER XXIX

THE ASIAGO PLATEAU 179

CHAPTER XXX

SOME NOTES ON NATIONAL CHARACTERISTICS . . . 193

CHAPTER XXXI

ROME IN THE SPRING 197

CHAPTER XXXII

THE FIFTEENTH OF JUNE, 1918 204

CHAPTER XXXIII

IN THE TRENTINO 214

CHAPTER XXXIV

PAGE
SIRMIONE AND SOLFERINO 222

CHAPTER XXXV

THE ASIAGO PLATEAU ONCE MORE 230

PART VI
THE LAST PHASE

CHAPTER XXXVI

THE MOVE TO THE PIAVE 236

CHAPTER XXXVII

THE BEGINNING OF THE LAST BATTLE 242

CHAPTER XXXVIII

ACROSS THE RIVER 246

CHAPTER XXXIX

LIBERATORI 252

CHAPTER XL

THE COMPLETENESS OF VICTORY 258

CHAPTER XLI

IN THE EUGANEAN HILLS 262

CHAPTER XLII

LAST THOUGHTS ON LEAVING ITALY 264

LIST OF ILLUSTRATIONS

ITALIAN TROOPS CROSSING A SNOWFIELD IN THE
TRENTINO . . . . *Frontispiece*

To face page

RAILWAY BRIDGE OVER THE ISONZO WRECKED BY AUSTRIAN
SHELL FIRE 56

ITALIAN MULE TRANSPORT ON THE CARSO . . . 70

NO. 3 GUN OF THE FIRST BRITISH BATTERY IN ITALY . 70

CASA GIRARDI AND ITALIAN HUTS 170

SOME OF OUR BATTERY HUTS NEAR CASA GIRARDI . 170

THE EASTERN PORTION OF THE ASIAGO PLATEAU . . 180

ROAD BEHIND OUR BATTERY POSITION LEADING TO PRIA
DELL' ACQUA 188

CHAPEL AT SAN SISTO AND ITALIAN GRAVES . . . 188

HUTS ON A MOUNTAIN SIDE IN THE TRENTINO . . 220

LORRIES LEAVING ASIAGO AFTER ITS LIBERATION . . 252

CAPTURED AUSTRIAN GUNS IN VAL D'ASSA . . . 252

LIST OF MAPS

MAP OF NORTHERN ITALY . . . . *Front Cover*

MAP OF THE ISONZO FRONT 24

MAP OF VAL BRENTA AND THE ASIAGO PLATEAU . . 162

WITH BRITISH GUNS IN ITALY

WITH
BRITISH GUNS IN ITALY

PART I
INTRODUCTORY

CHAPTER I

THE ANGLO-ITALIAN TRADITION AND ITALY'S PART IN THE WAR

ANGLO-ITALIAN friendship has been one of the few unchanging facts in modern international relations. Since the French Revolution, in the bellicose whirligig of history and of the old diplomacy's reckless dance with death, British troops have fought in turn against Frenchmen and Germans, against Russians and Austrians, against Bulgarians, Turks and Chinamen, against Boers, and even against Americans, but never, except for a handful of Napoleonic conscripts, against Italians. British and Italian troops, on the other hand, fought side by side in the Crimea, and, in the war which has just ended, have renewed and extended their comradeship in arms in Austria and Italy, in France and in the Balkans.

During the nineteenth century Italy in her Wars of Liberation gained, in a degree which this generation can hardly realise, the enthusiastic sympathy and the moral, and sometimes material, support of all the best elements in the British nation. There were poets—Byron and Shelley, the Brownings, Swinburne and Meredith—who were filled with a passionate devotion to the Italian cause.[1]   There were statesmen —Palmerston, Lord John Russell and Gladstone— who did good work for Italian freedom, and Italians still remember that in 1861 the British Government was the first to recognise the new Kingdom of United Italy, while the Governments of other Powers were intriguing to harass and destroy it.   There were individual, adventurous Englishmen, such as Forbes, the comrade of Garibaldi, who put their lives and their wealth at the disposal of Italian patriots.   But, beyond all these, it was the great mass of the British people which stood steadily behind the Italian people in its long struggle for unity and freedom.

Mazzini, Garibaldi and Cavour, " the soul, the sword and the brain," which together created Modern Italy, all had close personal relations with this country. Mazzini, driven from his own land by foreign oppressors, lived a great part of his life in exile among us, and here dreamed those dreams, which still inspire generous youth throughout the world.   When Garibaldi visited us in 1864, he was enthusiastically acclaimed by all sections of the nation, by the Prince of Wales, the Peerage and the Poet Laureate, no less than by the working classes.   It is recorded that, used as he was, as a soldier, to the roar of battle and, as a sailor, to the roar of the storm, Garibaldi almost quailed

---

[1] Even Tennyson, who was not very susceptible to foreign influences, invited Garibaldi to plant a tree in his garden.

before the tumultuous roar of welcome which greeted him as he came out of the railway station at Nine Elms. Cavour was a deep student and a great admirer of British institutions, both political and economic, and in a large measure founded Italian institutions upon them. And the first public speech he ever made was made in London in the English tongue.

These great men passed in time from the stage of Italian public life, and others took their places, but amid all the shifting complexities of recent international politics, no shadow has ever fallen across the path of Anglo-Italian friendship. And indeed during the Boer War Italy was the only friend we had left in Europe.

Italy's membership of the Triple Alliance was always subject to two conditions, first, that the Alliance was to be purely defensive, and second, that Italy would never support either of her partners in war against England. Thus, under the first condition, when Austria proposed in 1913 that the Triple Alliance should combine to crush Serbia, victorious but exhausted after the Balkan Wars, Italy at once rejected the proposal. And, under the second condition, as German naval expansion became more and more provocative and threatening to Britain, we were able to transfer nearly all our Mediterranean Fleet to the North Sea, secure in the knowledge that, whatever might befall, we should never find Italy among our enemies.

. . . . . .

The part which Italy has played during the war just ended, the great value of her contribution to the Allied cause, and the great sacrifices which that contribution has involved for her, have been often and admirably stated. But I doubt whether, even yet, these things are fully realised outside Italy, and I will, therefore, very shortly state them again.

When war broke out in August 1914, Italy declared her neutrality, on the ground that the war was aggressive on the part of the Central Powers, and that, therefore, the Triple Alliance no longer bound her. By her declaration of neutrality, she liberated the whole French Army to fight in Belgium and North-Eastern France, and rendered our sea communications with the East substantially secure. Bismarck used to say that, under the Triple Alliance, an Italian bugler and drummer boy posted on the Franco-Italian frontier would immobilise four French Army Corps. The Alliance disappointed the expectations of Bismarck's successors.

But if Italy had come in at this time on the German side, she might well have tilted swiftly and irremediably against us that awful equipoise of forces which, once established, lasted for more than four years. There would have been small hope that France, supported only by our small Expeditionary Force and faced with an Italian invasion in the South-East, in addition to a German invasion in the North-East, could have prevented the fall of Paris and the Channel Ports, while Austria, freed from all fear on the Italian frontier, perhaps even reinforced by part of the Italian Army, could have turned all her forces against Russia. Or alternatively, part of the Italian Army might have attacked Serbia through Austrian territory, with the probable result that Rumania and Greece, as well as

Bulgaria and Turkey, would have been brought in against us in the first month of the war.

At sea our naval supremacy would have been strained to breaking point by the many heavy tasks imposed upon it simultaneously in widely-separated seas. Our communications through the Mediterranean would, indeed, have been almost impossible to maintain.

Many bribes were offered to Italy at this time by the Central Powers in the hope of inducing her to join them—Corsica, Savoy and Nice, Tunis, Malta, and probably even larger rewards. But Italy remained neutral.

In May 1915 she entered the war on our side, in the first place to free those men of Italian race who still lived outside her frontiers, under grievous oppression, and whom Austria refused to give up to their Mother Country, and, in the second place, because already many Italians realised, as Americans also realised later, that the defeat of the Central Powers was a necessary first step towards the liberation of oppressed peoples everywhere and the building of a better world. Italy entered the war at a time when things were going badly for us in Russia, and looked very menacing in France, and when she herself was still ill-prepared for a long, expensive and exhausting struggle. The first effect of her entry was to pin down along the Alps and the Isonzo large Austrian forces, which would otherwise have been available for use elsewhere.

She entered the war nine months after the British Empire, but her losses, when the war ended, had been proportionately heavier than ours. According to the latest published information the total of Italian dead was 460,000 out of a population of 35 millions. The total of British dead for the whole British Empire, including Dominion, Colonial and Indian troops, was 670,000, and for the United Kingdom alone 500,000. The white population of the British Empire is 62 millions and of the United Kingdom 46 millions. Thus the Italian dead amount to more than 13 for every thousand of the population, and the British, whether calculated for the United Kingdom alone or for the whole white population of the Empire, to less than 11 for every thousand of the population. The long series of Battles of the Isonzo,—the journalists counted up to twelve of them in the first twenty-seven months in which Italy was at war,—the succession of offensives " from Tolmino to the sea," which were only dimly realised in England and France, cost Italy the flower of her youth. The Italian Army was continually on the offensive during those months against the strongest natural defences to be found in any of the theatres of war. On countless occasions Italian heroes went forth on forlorn hopes to scale and capture impossible precipices; and sometimes they succeeded. Through that bloody series of offensives the Italians slowly but steadily gained ground, and drew ever nearer to Trento and Trieste. Only those who went out to the Italian Front before Caporetto, and saw with their own eyes what the Italian Army had accomplished on the Carso and among the Julian Alps, can fully realise the greatness of the Italian effort.

It must never be forgotten that Italy is both the youngest and the poorest of the Great Powers of

Europe. Barely half a century has passed since United Italy was born, and the political and economic difficulties of her national childhood were enormous. For many years, as one of her own historians says, she was "not a state, but only the outward appearance of a state." Her natural resources are poor and limited. She possesses neither coal nor iron, and is still partially dependent on imported food and foreign shipping. She is still very poor in accumulated capital, and the burden of her taxation is very heavy.

From the moment of her entry into the war her economic problems became very difficult, especially that of the provision of guns and munitions in sufficient quantities, and the extent to which she solved this last problem is deserving of the greatest admiration. Her position grew even more difficult in 1917. After the military collapse of Russia she had to face practically the whole Austrian Army, instead of only a part of it, and a greatly increased weight of guns. The Austrians had 53 millions of population to draw from, the Italians only 35. Moreover, just before Caporetto, a number of German Divisions, with a powerful mass of artillery and aircraft, were thrown into the Austrian scale, while from the Italian was withdrawn the majority of that tiny handful of French and British Batteries, which were all the armed support which, up to that time, her Allies had ever lent her. Only five British Batteries and a few French were left on the Italian Front. By the defeat of Caporetto she lost a great quantity of guns and stores and practically the whole of her Second Army, while half of Venetia fell into the hands of the enemy, and remained in his possession for a year. The inferiority of the Italian

Army to its enemies, both in numbers and in material, was thus sharply increased.

But the Italians held grimly on; they turned at bay on the Piave and in the mountains, and checked the onrush of Austrians and Germans. Then, supported by French and British reinforcements, but still inferior in numbers, they continued for a year longer to hold up almost the whole strength of Austria. That winter the poor were very near starvation in the cities of Italy, and the peasants had to cut down their olive groves for fuel. The following spring part of the French and British reinforcements were withdrawn to France, together with an Italian contingent which numerically balanced the French and British who remained in Italy.

The Austrians also lost their German support and sent some of their own troops to France, but they retained their numerical superiority on the Italian Front. In June they launched a great attack on a seventy-mile front, which was to have made an end of Italy; but the Italians beat them back. Then four months later, after an intense effort of preparation, Italy, still inferior in numbers and material, struck for the last time and utterly destroyed the Austrian Army in the great battle which will be known to history as Vittorio Veneto. The Austrians lost twice as many prisoners and four times as many guns at Vittorio Veneto as they had taken at Caporetto.

The war on the Italian Front was over, the Austrian Army was broken beyond recovery, the Austrian State was dissolving into its national elements, which only tradition, corruption and brute force had for so

long held together. Italy, heroic and constant, had
endured to the end, and with her last great gesture
had both completed her own freedom, and given their
freedom to those who had been the instruments of
her enemies.

PART II

SOME EARLY IMPRESSIONS

CHAPTER II

FROM FOLKESTONE TO VENICE

ON the 6th July, 1917, I arrived at Folkestone armed with a War Office letter ordering my " passage to France for reinforcements for Siege Artillery Batteries in Italy." I had a millpond crossing in the afternoon, and that evening left Boulogne for Modane.

Next morning at 2 a.m. I was awakened from frowsy sleep by a French soldier, laden with baggage, who stumbled headlong into the railway carriage which I was sharing with three other British officers. We were at Amiens. I was last here ten months before, when my Division was coming back from rest to fight a second time upon the Somme. I did not sleep again, but watched the sunrise behind an avenue of poplars, as we passed through Creil, and the woods of Chantilly shining wonderfully in the early morning light. I spent that day in Paris and left again in the evening.

Next morning, the 8th, I awoke at Bourg in High Savoy. Here too the poplar dominates in the valleys. We ran along the shores of Lake Bourget and up the beautiful valley of the Arc in misty rain. We arrived at Modane at 10 a.m., and I was booked through to Palmanova, a new name to me at that time. The train left an hour later and, as we lunched, we passed through the Mont Cenis tunnel and slid rapidly downwards through Alpine valleys, charming enough but less beautiful than those on the French side of the frontier. Very soon it became perceptibly warmer, electric fans were set in motion and ice was served with the wine.

I found that I had six hours to wait at Turin before the train left for Milan. My fleeting impression of Turin was of a very well-planned city, its Corsi spacious and well shaded with trees, its trams multitudinous, its many distant vistas of wooded hills and of the Superga Palace beyond the Po a delight to the eye. But I found less animation there than I had expected, except in a church, where a priest was ferociously declaiming and gesticulating at a perspiring crowd, mostly women, who were patiently fanning themselves in the stifling, unventilated heat. I was an object of interest in the streets, where the British uniform was not yet well known. Some took me for a Russian and some little boys ran after me and asked for a rouble. A group of women agreed that I was Spanish.

The train for Milan goes right through to Venice, so, being momentarily independent of the British military authorities, I decided to spend a few hours there on my way to the Front.

The carriage was full of Italian officers, chiefly Cavalry, Flying Corps and Infantry. It is their custom on meeting an unknown officer of their own or of an Allied Army to stand stiffly upright, to shake hands and introduce themselves by name. This little

ceremony breaks the ice. I saw many of them also
on the platforms and in the corridor of the train. The
majority, especially of their mounted officers, are very
elegant and many very handsome, and they have
those charming easy manners which are everywhere
characteristic of the Latin peoples.

Nearly all Italian officers speak French. In their
Regular Army French and either English or German
are compulsory studies, and a good standard of fluent
conversation is required. In these early days my
Italian was rather broken, so we talked mostly French.
At Milan all my companions except one got out, and
a new lot got in. But I was growing sleepy, and after
the formal introductions I began to drowse.

. . . . . .

I woke several times in the night and early morning,
and, half asleep, looked out through the carriage
window upon wonderful sights. A railway platform
like a terrace in a typical Italian garden, ornate with
a row of carved stone vases of perfect form, and vines
in festoons from vase to vase, and dark trees behind,
and then a downward slope and little white houses
asleep in the distance. This I think was close to
Brescia. Then Desenzano, and what I took to be
the distant glimmer of Lake Garda under the stars.
Verona I passed in my sleep, having now crossed the
boundary of Lombardy into Venetia, and Vicenza and
Padua are nothing from the train. At Mestre, the
junction for the Front, all the Italian officers got out,
and I went on to Venice.

Except for three British Naval officers I was, I
think, the only foreigner there, and a priest, whom I
met, took me for an American. Everything of value

in Venice, that could be, was sandbagged now for fear of bombs, and much that was movable had been taken away. I spent three hours in a gondola on the Grand Canal and up and down the Rii, filled with a dreamy amazement, at the superb harmonies of form and colour of things both far away and close at hand. And even as seen in war-time, with all the accustomed life of Venice broken and spoiled, the spaciousness of the Piazza S. Marco, and the beauty of the buildings that stand around it, and at night the summer lightnings, and a rainstorm, and a café under the colonnade, where music was being played, will linger always in my memory. All the big hotels were closed now, or taken over by the Government as offices or hospitals, and the gondolas lay moored in solitary lines along the Grand Canal, and even the motor boats were few and, as a waiter said to me, " no one has been here for three years, but the people are very quiet and no one complains."

CHAPTER III

FROM VENICE TO THE ISONZO FRONT

I LEFT Venice next morning by the 5.55 train, and reached Palmanova at half-past ten. As one goes eastward by this railway, there is a grand panorama of hills, circling the whole horizon ; to the north and north-east the Carnic Alps and Cadore, their highest summits crowned with snow even in the full heat of summer ; eastward the Julian Alps, beyond the Isonzo, stretching from a point north of

Tolmino, down behind the Carso, almost to Fiume in the south-east ; and yet further round the circle to the southward the mountains of Istria, running behind Trieste and its wide blue gulf, whose waters are invisible from this railway across the plain.

Of Palmanova I will write again. This was the Railhead and the Ammunition Dump for the British Batteries. I stayed there that day scarcely an hour, and then went on by motor lorry to Gradisca, the Headquarters of " British Heavy Artillery, Italy." Here I lunched and was well received by the Staff, who were expecting no reinforcements and were astonished at my coming. It was decided, after some discussion, to attach me temporarily to a Battery which had one officer in hospital, slightly wounded by shrapnel. I continued my journey in another motor lorry after lunch. Gradisca lies on the western bank of the Isonzo, which is crossed close by at Peteano by a magnificent broad wooden bridge, the work of Italian engineers. Gradisca had not been badly damaged, the Austrians having made no great resist-ance here against the Italian advance in May 1915, but Peteano had been laid absolutely flat by Austrian twelve-inch guns. It had been utterly destroyed in half an hour's intense bombardment some months before, and many Italian hutments in the neighbour-hood had been destroyed at the same time.

Within sight of this bridge, at a distance of a quarter of a mile, is the confluence of the Vippacco with the Isonzo. From this point the road follows the Vippacco to Rubbia, the Headquarters of Colonel Raven, who commanded the Northern Group of British Batteries, which I was now joining. The five Batteries of this Group, known as "B 2," were all in positions on or near the Vippacco, firing on the northern edge of the Carso, and eastward along the river valley. The southern Group, "B 1," were on the Carso itself and operating chiefly against the famous Hermada, a position of tremendous natural strength, directly covering Trieste. B 2 had the more comfortable and better-shaded positions, but B 1, though their guns were among the rocks and in the full heat of the sun, were in easy reach of the sea, and had a Rest Camp at Grado among the lagoons.

Raven's Group, B 2, formed part of an Italian Raggruppamento, or collection of Groups, under the command of a certain Sicilian Colonel named Canale, a dapper little man who generally wore white gloves, even in the front line. He was a fearless and capable officer and did all in his power for the comfort of our Batteries.

From Rubbia I drove in a car to the Battery. As I left the Group Headquarters, a number of wooden huts at the foot of the wooded slopes of Monte San Michele, which rise upwards from the road, I went under the railway which in peace-time connects Gorizia with Trieste. It is useless now, being within easy range of the Austrian guns, which have, moreover, broken down the high stone bridge on which the line crosses the Vippacco. A young Sicilian Sergeant accompanied me as a guide and pointed out Gorizia, some six miles away to the north, a widely-scattered town, very white in the sunlight, lying at the foot of high hills famous in the history of the war on this Front, Monte Sabotino, Monte Santo, Monte San

Gabriele, of which there will be more for me to say
hereafter.

The gun positions of my new Battery were situated
just outside the little village of Pec, inhabited mostly
by Slovene peasantry before the war, now all vanished.
The village had been much shelled, first by Italian
and then by Austrian guns, and there was not a house
remaining undamaged, though several had been
patched up as billets and cookhouses by British troops.
Another of our Batteries had their guns actually in
the ruins of the village, but ours were alongside a
sunken road, leading down to the Vippacco. The guns
themselves were concealed in thick bowers of acacias,
the branches of which had been clipped here and there
within our arc of fire. I doubt if anywhere, on any
Front, a British Battery occupied a position of greater
natural beauty. The officers' Mess and sleeping huts
were a few hundred yards from the guns, right on the
bank of the Vippacco, likewise hidden from view and
shaded from the sun by a great mass of acacias, a
luxuriant soft roof of fresh green leaves. Our Mess,
indeed, had no other roof than this, for there was seldom
any rain, and, as we sat at meals, we faced a broad
waterfall, a curving wall of white foam, stretching
right across the stream, which was at this point about
seventy or eighty yards wide. Innumerable blue
dragon-flies flitted backwards and forwards in the
sunlight. Though the weather was warm, it was less
hot than usual at this time of year, and the surroundings of our Mess reminded me vividly of Kerry. In
the first days that followed I could often imagine
myself back in beautiful and familiar places in the
south-west corner of Ireland. Only Italian gunners

coming and going, for several of their Battery positions
were close to ours, and the Castello di Rubbia across
the water, slightly but not greatly damaged, broke
this occasional illusion.

These Italians took us quite for granted now, and
that evening I began to learn about their Front.
Things were pretty quiet at present on both sides,
but greater activity was expected soon. I made the
acquaintance of Venosta, an Italian Artillery officer
attached to the Battery. He was from Milan, a
member of a well-known Lombard family, and had
a soft and quiet way with him and a certain supple
charm. At ordinary times he preferred to take things
easily, and was imperturbable by anything which he
thought unimportant. But in crises, as I learned later
on, he could show much calm resource and energy.

.   .   .   .   .   .

I woke next morning to the sound of the Vippacco
waterfall, and the following day I got my first real
impression of this part of the Italian Front. The
Battery was doing a registration shoot and I went up
in the afternoon with our Second-in-Command to
an O.P. on the top of the Nad Logem to observe and
correct our fire. It was a great climb, up a stony
watercourse, now dry, and then through old Austrian
trenches, elaborately blasted in the Carso rock and
captured a year ago. The Nad Logem is part of the
northern edge of the Carso, and from our O.P. a
great panorama spread out north, east and west, with
the sinuous Vippacco in the foreground, fringed with
trees. From here I had pointed out to me the various
features of the country. The play of light and shade
in the distance was very wonderful. Our target that

2

afternoon was a point in the Austrian front line on a
long, low, brown hill lying right below us, known
officially as Hill 126.   The Austrians some days before
had sent us an ironical wireless message, " We have
evacuated Hill 94 and Hill 126 for a week so that
the British Batteries may register on them." They
evidently knew something of our whereabouts and our
plans !

Coming back we stopped at the foot of a hill on
which stands the shell-wrecked monastery of San
Grado di Merna, a white ruin gaunt against the darker
background of the Nad Logem.   Here a new Battery
position was being prepared for us, only three hundred
yards behind the Austrian front line, but admirably
protected by the configuration of the ground from
enemy fire.   An Italian drilling machine was at work
here, operated by compressed air, drilling holes in the
rock for the insertion of dynamite charges, and, by
means of gradual blasting, gun pits and cartridge
recesses and dug-outs were being created in the
stubborn rock.   Here a heavy thunderstorm broke
and we sheltered in the Headquarters of an Italian
Field Artillery Brigade, likewise blasted out of the
mountain side.   I returned with Venosta.   I asked
him to show me the famous Bersagliere trot, and by
way of illustration we doubled along the road for about
half a mile.   On the British Front the spectacle of
two officers thus disporting themselves for no apparent
reason would have caused much remark and amusement.   But the Italians, whom we passed, seemed to
see nothing remarkable in our behaviour.   They are,
perhaps, more tolerant of eccentricity than we are.

. . . . . .

It may be of interest at this point to say a few words about some of the special characteristics of the Italian Army. Every modern Army has adopted a distinctive colour for its war-time uniform, chosen with a view to minimising visibility. Thus we wear khaki, the French horizon-blue, the Germans field-grey. The Italians have adopted an olive colour, commonly spoken of as " grigio-verde," or grey-green.

The various Italian Corps, Regiments and Brigades wear distinctively coloured collars on their tunics which, except in the case of the Arditi, fit closely round the neck. For example, the Granatieri, or Grenadiers, who both in their high physical standards and military prestige resemble our own Guards Battalions, wear a collar of crimson and white. The colour of the Artillery is black with a yellow border, that of the Engineers black with a red border. Of the Infantry, the Alpini collars are green and the Bersaglieri crimson, the bands of colour being shaped in each case like sharp-pointed flames turning outwards. For this reason the Alpini are often called the " fiamme verdi," or green flames, and the Bersaglieri " fiamme rosse," or red flames. The Infantry Brigades of the line, who bear local names,—the Avellino Brigade, the Como Brigade, the Lecce Brigade and so forth,—have each their distinctively coloured collars.

These local names mean very little, for, as a matter of policy, men from all parts of Italy are mixed indiscriminately together in each Brigade. The Parma Brigade, for example, will contain only a few men from Parma, and them by chance. One of the objects of this policy is to help to break down those regional barriers, which still linger owing to historical causes,

between different districts of Italy. It is often re-
marked that men from many parts of Italy know more
of foreign countries than of other parts of their own
country, and most of the numerous local dialects are
hardly intelligible to men who live far from the
districts where they are spoken. Ordinary Italian,
which is in fact the local dialect of Rome, is, as it were,
the *lingua franca* of the whole country, but the great
majority of Italians speak not only Italian but one,
or sometimes several, local dialects, and the latter
are used by all classes in their own homes. Some of
these dialects differ widely from Italian. In many
remote districts some of the peasants cannot speak
Italian at all.

The Alpini and the two Sardinian Brigades, Cagliari
and Sassari, are exceptions to the rule mentioned
above. The Alpini are in peace-time recruited entirely from the men who dwell in the Alps, though I
believe that during the present war a certain number
of men from the Apennines have also been included
in Alpini Battalions. The Alpini are specially used
for warfare in the mountains. They wear in their
hats a single long feather. Closely attached to the
Alpini are the Mountain Artillery, armed with light
guns of about the same calibre as our own twelve-
pounders. They too are recruited from the moun-
taineers and wear the Alpino hat and single feather.
The Alpini have a magnificent regimental spirit and,
in my judgment, are the equals of any troops in the
world.

The Cagliari and Sassari Brigades, two of the best
in the Italian Army, are composed entirely of Sardinians.
When in the front line they use the Sardinian dialect

on the telephone. Even if the Austrians succeed,
by means of "listening sets," in overhearing them,
it hardly matters, for it is not likely that anyone in
the Austrian front line will understand !

The Bersaglieri, another famous Italian Regiment,
are recruited from all parts of Italy, but only from
men of high physical fitness. They correspond roughly
to the Light Infantry of other Armies, and always
drill and march to a very quick step, even when
carrying machine guns on their shoulders. Their
hats decked with a mass of green cocks' feathers
are familiar in illustrations. The Bersagliere Cyclist
Companies, used for scouting purposes, form part
of the Regiment. The Bersagliere undress cap is
a red fez with a blue tassel.

The Arditi, or Assault Detachments, correspond
to the German Sturmtruppen. They were instituted
in the Italian Army in 1917. They also consist
of picked men, and undergo a special training to
accustom them to bomb-throwing at close quarters
and to other incidents of the assault. In the course
of this training casualties often occur. Only young
unmarried men of exceptionally good physique can
become Arditi. They are only used in actual attacks
and never for the purpose of merely holding trenches.
They therefore spend a large part of their time behind
the lines and receive, I believe, extra pay and rations.
They are armed with rifles and *pugnali*, or small
daggers, and wear a low-cut tunic, with a black knot-
tie and a black fez. On each lapel of their tunic
they wear two black flames, similar to the crimson
flames on the collars of the Bersaglieri. They are,
therefore, known as " fiamme nere," or black flames.

A large proportion of Arditi are Sicilians, and their fighting quality is very high. Certain detachments of Bersaglieri are also classified as Assault Detachments and wear low-cut tunics like the Arditi.

The Italian Mountain and Field Artillery are excellent; their Heavy Artillery is handicapped, in comparison with ours, by its smaller ammunition supply and fewer opportunities for prolonged practice, but its methods are scientific and its personnel very keen and capable. The Italian Engineers have done much wonderful work, to which I shall refer later.

CHAPTER IV

THE WAR ON THE ISONZO FRONT

FROM Monte Nero to the Adriatic the distance is, in a straight line, some 35 miles. Allowing for the curves of the actual line, the length of Front is between 40 and 50 miles. This portion of the Italian and Austrian lines is commonly spoken of as the Isonzo Front. It is not like the Front in the higher Alps, where, as on the Adamello, trenches are cut in the solid ice, where the firing of a single gun may precipitate an avalanche, where more Italians are killed by avalanches than by Austrians, where guns have to be dragged up precipices and perched on ledges fit only, one might think, for an eagle's nest, where food, ammunition, reinforcements, wounded and sick have all to travel in small cages attached to wire ropes, slung from peak to peak above sheer drops of many thousand feet, where sentries have to stand rigidly stationary, so as to remain invisible, and have to be changed every ten minutes owing to the intense cold, where.Battalions of Alpini charge down snow slopes on skis at the rate of thirty miles an hour, where refraction and the deceiving glare of the snow make accurate rifle fire impossible even for crack shots,—the Isonzo Front is not so astounding and impossible a Front as this, but it is yet a very different Front from any on which British troops are elsewhere fighting in this war.

It is a country with a strange beauty of its own; it is, in its own measure, rough and mountainous, and it is within sight of other and loftier mountains to the north-west. At my first view of it I remembered a speech of Carlo, the hero of Meredith's *Vittoria*, concerning Lombard cities away on the other side of the Trentino, " Brescia under the big Eastern hill which throws a cloak on it at sunrise ! Brescia is always the eagle's nest that looks over Lombardy ! And Bergamo ! You know the terraces of Bergamo. Aren't they like a morning sky ? Dying there is not death ; it's flying into the dawn. You Romans envy us. You have no Alps, no crimson hills, nothing but old walls to look on while you fight. Farewell, Merthyr Powys. . . ." To me those words were always recurring on the Italian Front. " Dying here is not death ; it's flying into the dawn." I would have liked to have them engraved on my tombstone, if Fate had set one up for me in this land, whose beauty casts a spell on all one's senses.

.   .   .   .   .   .

The Isonzo Front is divided into two parts by the

Vippacco river, which flows roughly from east to west and joins the Isonzo at Peteano. Of these two parts the northern is three times as long as the southern. The northern part was held by the Italian Second Army, under General Capello, the southern by the Italian Third Army, under the Duke of Aosta. In the north the Isonzo runs through a deep ravine, with Monte Nero rising on its eastern side. Monte Nero is some 6800 feet high. The Alpini took it by a marvellous feat of mountain warfare in the first year of the war. South of Monte Nero, also on the east bank of the river, lies the town of Tolmino, the object of many fierce Italian assaults, but not yet taken. Here the Isonzo bends south-westward and continues to flow through a deep ravine past Canale and Plava, with the Bainsizza Plateau rising on its eastern bank. This Plateau is of a general height of about 2400 feet, and is continued south-eastward by the Ternova Plateau, rising to a general height of about 2200 feet. Bending again towards the south-east, the Isonzo flows out into the Plain of Gorizia. Here stand Monte Sabotino and Monte Santo, the western and eastern pillars of this gateway leading into the lower lands. East of Monte Santo, along the southern edge of the Plateau, stand Monte San Gabriele and Monte San Daniele. Here the Plateau falls precipitously down to the Vippacco valley, only the long brown foothill of San Marco breaking the drop.

Gorizia has scattered suburbs : Salcano to the north, in the very mouth of the gorge, the fashionable suburb in days before the war ; Podgora to the west, on the other side of the Isonzo, industrial,

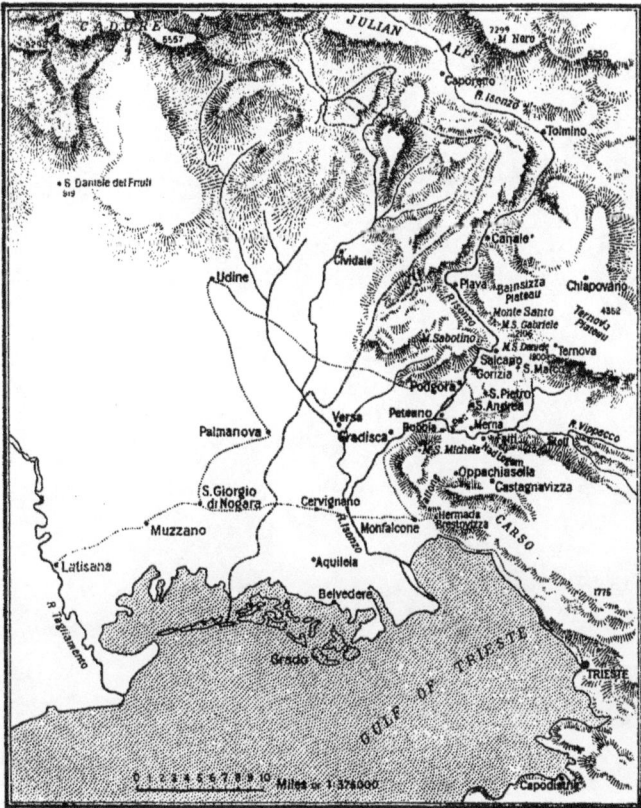

THE ISONZO FRONT

under the shadow of Podgora Hill, which is a continuation south-westwards of Monte Sabotino ; San Pietro and Sant' Andrea to the south, agricultural but containing a few villas. Below Gorizia the Isonzo continues through the plain south-westward, past its junction with the Vippacco, past Gradisca on its western bank, past Monfalcone, and then south-eastward again till it reaches the marshes of Punta Sdobba and flows into the Gulf of Trieste. On the southern side of the Vippacco valley are the foothills of the Carso, brown and infertile, with a few shattered pine trees. To the south of these rises a long line of hills, the real northern edge of the Carso, from Stoll on the east to Dosso Faiti, sloping down to the Volconiac, and the Nad Logem and Velichi. Most of these hillsides are covered with stone pines. To the south of them stretches the Carso proper, barren, treeless, waterless, "the inexorable Carso," as the Italians call it, with a few little squalid villages, of which Castagnevizza and Oppachiasella, where Francis Joseph had a hunting-box, are the largest. It is threaded by the shallow valley of Brestovizza, to the south of which rises the great hump of the Hermada, an almost impregnable natural barrier. To the south of this again lies the little town of Duino on the sea. Immediately west of the Carso runs the Vallone, which at the time of my arrival was a hive of huts and a great artery of traffic from north to south, and west of the Vallone rises Monte San Michele, for the possession of which the first big battle on this Front was fought.

·   ·   ·   ·   ·   ·   ·

The Isonzo Front was the only possible field for an Italian offensive on a great scale, and the possession of the Carso, of the Bainsizza and Ternova Plateaus and of Monte Nero are as essential to the future security of the Venetian Plain as the possession of the Trentino itself. The frontiers of northern and north-eastern Italy were drawn according to the methods of the old diplomacy after the war of 1866, when Bismarck, seeking to keep Austria neutral in the next war on his schedule, that with France, willingly sacrificed the interests of his Italian Allies. For half a century Lombardy and Venetia have lived under the continual threat of an Austrian descent from the mountains, both from the Trentino, thrust like a wedge into the heart of Northern Italy, and across the Isonzo from the east. Nor has this threat been remote. When Italy was plunged in grief at the time of the Messina earthquake, the Austrian General Staff almost persuaded their Government that the moment had come to strike her down into the dust, and recover Lombardy and Venetia for Francis Joseph and Rome for the Pope. And so to-day an Italian Army fighting on the Isonzo Front fights in continual danger of having its line of communications cut by an Austrian offensive from the Trentino.

The population of the Trentino is indisputably Italian. East of the Isonzo the people are mainly Italian in the towns and mainly Slovene in the country districts. It has been the deliberate policy of the Austrian Government to plant new Slovene colonies here from time to time and to render life intolerable for Italians. But, even so, the population is still sparse, and all the country is infertile, except for the Vippacco Valley, which, though wretchedly cultivated hitherto, would richly repay the application of capital and modern methods. Here, I think, is a clear case where strategic considerations, which are definite, must prevail over racial considerations, which are dubious. These lands must be Italian after the war, if, with even the dimmest possibility of war remaining, Italians are to have peace of mind. Nor does a strong defensive frontier for Italy here imply a weak defensive frontier for her eastern neighbours. For the tangle of mountains continues for many miles further east.

. . . . . .

Venosta told me that, when they took San Michele in July 1916, the Italians lost 7000 in killed alone, seasoned soldiers of their old Army, whom it has been hard to replace. But when San Michele fell, they swept on and took Gorizia and all the surrounding plain at one bound, and, in the same offensive, Monte Sabotino. This victory has a special significance in modern Italian history, for it was the first time that an Army composed of men from all parts of United Italy fought a pitched battle against a great Army of Austria, Italy's secular enemy and oppressor. Monte Cucco and Monte Vodice were taken in the offensive of May 1917, and here, as at Monte Nero, the Alpini performed feats of arms which, to soldiers accustomed to fighting on the flat, must seem all but incredible. In one case twenty Alpini climbed up a sheer rock face at night by means of ropes, and leaping upon the Austrian sentries killed and threw them over the cliff without a sound, so that, when the main body of Alpini, climbing by hardly less difficult paths, reached the summit, they took the Austrian garrison in the rear and by surprise, and the heights were theirs.

Monte Santo was still Austrian when I came, though the Italians held trenches half-way up. On the summit the white ruins of a famous convent were clearly visible. Here some of the bloodiest Infantry fighting of the whole war took place in May 1917. The Italians were on the top once in the full flood of that offensive, but could not hold it. Four gallant Battalions charged up those steep slopes only to find that the Artillery preparation had been insufficient and that the convent wall had not been destroyed. Austrians poured out from deep caverns in the rock, where they had taken refuge during the bombardment, and threw down bombs from the top of the wall upon the Italians below. For these there was no way round and no question of retreat, so they all died where they stood, struggling to climb a wall thirty feet high, clambering upon one another's shoulders.

South of the Vippacco we held the Volconiac and Dosso Faiti, but not Hill 464, though this had been taken and lost again, nor yet the hills further east, nor any of the northern foothills of the Carso, except Hill 123. To the south again the Hermada had proved a great and bloody obstacle.

.   .   .   .   .   .

Three striking characteristics of the warfare on this Front impressed themselves upon my mind—first, the shortage of ammunition ; second, the enormous natural strength of all the Austrian positions; third, the work of the Italian Engineers.

Judged by the standards of warfare in France and Flanders, both Italians and Austrians were very short of ammunition. For Italy, a young and poor country, possessing neither coal nor iron and thrown largely on her own resources for manufacturing munitions of war, this was no matter of surprise. It was astonishing that the Italian Artillery was so well supplied as it was. But, to bring out the contrast, one may note that, whereas in Italy " fuoco normale " for Siege Artillery was six rounds per gun per hour, in France at this time a British Siege Battery's " ordinary " was thirty rounds per gun per hour. And one may note further that the number of Siege Batteries on a given length of Front in France was, even at this time, more than four times as great as the corresponding number on the Italian Front. The Austrians to some extent made up for their small quantity of guns and shells by a high proportion of guns of large calibre. Their twelve-inch howitzers were disagreeably numerous. It resulted, however, that neither Italians nor Austrians could afford to indulge in continuous heavy bombardments, such as were the rule in France. There was here on neither side a surplus of shell to fire away at targets of secondary importance, and therefore there was less destruction than in France of towns and villages near the lines. Ammunition had to be accumulated for important occasions and important targets. Thus battles were still separate and distinct in Italy, with perceptible intervals of lull, less apt than in France to become one blurred series of gigantic

actions. So too counter-battery work on a great
scale was not practised on either side out here, partly
for reasons of ammunition supply, and partly for
technical reasons connected with the nature of the
ground. For in a good *caverna* one was perfectly
safe, though outside high explosive produced not
only its own natural effect, but also a shower of
pieces of rock, thus combining the unpleasant characteristics of high explosive and shrapnel. One of
our gunners had his ribs broken by a blow from a
large piece of rock, though standing three hundred
yards away from where the shell burst. But often
after a heavy bombardment it was found that the
enemy had been sitting quietly in *caverne*, ready
to emerge with his machine guns when the attacking Infantry advanced. Aeroplanes also were less
numerous than in France. And, when I arrived,
gas was not much employed on either side.

In the second place, I was deeply impressed with
the natural strength of the Austrians' positions.
Almost everywhere they held high ground. On no
other Front in this war have stronger positions been
carried by assault than San Michele, Sabotino, Cucco,
Vodice, Monte Nero, and, in the end, Monte Santo.
No one who has not seen with his own eyes the
heights which Italian Infantry have conquered, backed
by no great Artillery support, can realise the astounding things which the Italians have performed. The
Italian Infantry have died in masses, with high hearts
and in the exaltation of delirium, crumpled, rent and
agonised, achieving the impossible.

And in the third place I would say something of
the work of their Engineers. Italian Engineers are

famous all the world over, but they have done nothing more magnificent than their swift building of innumerable roads, broad and well-laid and with marvellously easy gradients, both in these inhospitable and undeveloped border lands beside the Isonzo, and along the whole mountain Front. They have made possible troop movements and a regular system of supply under the most difficult conditions. It is a work worthy of the descendants of the old Romans, who by their road building laid the foundations of civilisation throughout Western Europe. And only second to their road making, I would place the work of the Italian Engineers in blasting *caverne* and gun positions and trenches in the rock, an invaluable and unending labour.

.   .   .   .   .   .

We British Gunners spent our first Italian summer in khaki drill tunics and shorts [1] and Australian " smasher hats." When these hats were first issued, one Battery Commander declared them to be " unsoldierly " in appearance and asked for permission to return them to the Ordnance. But this was not allowed. The men stood the heat well, though at the beginning, before they had got accustomed to the change of climate, there was some dysentery. I myself, a few days after my arrival and before I had a smasher hat, had a touch of the sun and lay about all day cursing the flies. But next day I was all right again.

Our rations at this time were a special Anglo-Italian blend ; less meat, bacon, cheese and tea than

---

[1] Next summer the introduction of mustard gas made it unsafe to leave our knees uncovered.

in the British ration, but macaroni, rice, coffee, wine and lemons from the Italian. It was a good ration and no one suffered from eating a little less meat than at home. In order to check the spread of dysentery, it was ordered by the medical authorities that no meat was to be eaten at midday.

We were not doing a great deal of firing when I came, though we had always to be prepared to come suddenly and quickly into action, especially at night. Most of our prearranged daylight shoots were observed from an O.P. in a ruined house at S. Andrea, on the plain just outside Gorizia, where one had a fine view southwards of the Tamburo and of the whole boundary ridge of the Carso from Dosso Faiti to the Stoll. Observation was beautifully easy on these high hills and in this clear air. What worlds away is this country with its wonderful cloudless sunshine from the dismal flat lands of the Western Front! Said one enthusiast of ours, "This is a gunner's heaven!" The Austrians fancied, I think, that we had our O.P. in Vertoiba, which is north of S. Andrea, for they shelled this frequently, but S. Andrea seldom. They shelled Vertoiba heavily, I remember, all one afternoon, while I was on duty at S. Andrea and while the Italian Staff were present in large numbers for two hours to watch our shooting. I remember thinking what a fine bag they would have got if they had lifted about four hundred yards! The Italian Staff were always most complimentary and enthusiastic over the work of our Batteries.

We had taken part in the Italian May offensive, the results of which had been claimed by the *Daily Mail*, with characteristic good taste and sense of proportion, as a " great Anglo-Italian victory." Our part had been more justly described by General Cadorna, who in a special Order of the Day had said that " amid the roar of battle was clearly heard the voice of British guns," and in his summary of the results of this offensive, which lasted from May 12th to May 30th, after remarking that the number of Austrians taken prisoners was 23,681 men and 604 officers, and that, in addition, at least 100,000 Austrians had been put out of action, continued as follows, " Our brave Infantry fought indefatigably for eighteen days, without pause and without proper food supplies, on difficult ground, in almost mid-summer heat, impetuous in attack and tenacious in defence. Most effective at all times was the fraternal co-operation of the Artillery, Siege, Field or Mountain, one Field Battery not hesitating to push right up to the firing line. Excellent help, too, was lent by ten Batteries of medium calibre of the British Army and by the guns of the Italian Navy."

Cadorna had inspected our Batteries soon after their arrival in Italy, and we had been visited and officially welcomed on behalf of the Italian Government by the Minister Bissolati, perhaps the most vivid and vital personality in Italian politics, and a wise counsellor, whose advice has more than once been disastrously ignored.[1]

---

[1] From the outbreak of war in August 1914, Bissolati strongly advocated Italian intervention on the side of the Allies. When Italy declared war, he enlisted in the ranks of the Alpini, although over military age, was decorated for valour and seriously wounded. He then became Minister for Military Supplies, and acted as a connecting link between the Cabinet at Rome and the High Command.

3

Addressing at Pec detachments from a number of British Batteries on the 29th of May, Bissolati had said : "Officers and men of the British Force, I bring you the greetings of the Italian Government and the thanks of the Italian people. I greet you not only as an Italian Minister, but as a comrade in arms, for I consider it the greatest privilege of my life to have been in this war a soldier like yourselves. Our hearts beat with joy to see you here, because there is no Italian, however humble his station, who does not know how great is the debt of Italy to Britain for the brotherly help afforded her during the tragic vicissitudes of the glorious story of her Resurrection. We all remember how your fathers helped to create the Italian nation. . . . To-day we find ourselves fighting side by side in the same campaign, we to redeem this territory from the Austrian yoke, you to maintain the liberty of your national existence from the German menace, both of us, moreover, to set the whole world free from the peril of falling under the dominion of that race, hard in temper as a granite rock, which finds in the Austro-Hungarian Empire a willing ally in its rapes and aggressions. I am here, then, to thank you, not only as an Italian, but as a man, and I am filled with joy at the thought that the British, even as the Italians, are showing themselves to be, now as always, the champions of justice, and the defenders of liberty and right. The sacrifices which we are making together, the mingling of our blood upon the battle-field, will render even stronger the agelong, traditional friendship between our two nations.

Viva l'Inghilterra !   Viva l'Italia ! "

CHAPTER V

PALMANOVA

DURING my first month in Italy I lived a nomadic life. I was only "attached" to a Battery, and really nobody's child. July 17th to 22nd I spent at Palmanova in charge of an Artillery fatigue party which was helping the Ordnance to load and unload ammunition, and from August 2nd to 10th I was in charge of another working party of gunners at Versa, a fly-bitten, dusty little village, which our medical authorities had stupidly selected as a site for a Hospital, though there were many suitable villas in more accessible and agreeable places not far away. But in this first month I was lucky in being able to multiply and vary my impressions of the Eastern Veneto.

.   .   .   .   .   .

I rode down to Palmanova from Gradisca on a motor lorry. What a country! The white houses, the white roads, the masses of fresh green foliage, chiefly acacias, the tall dark cypresses, the cool blue water of the Isonzo, the blue-grey mountains in the distance, and on their summits the sunshine on the snow, which is hardly distinguishable from the low-lying cloud banks in an otherwise cloudless sky.

Italian troops, dusty columns marching along the road, throw up at me an occasional greeting as the lorry goes by. Long lines of transport pass continually. "Sempre Avanti Savoia!" "Sempre Avanti Italia!" I find my eyes wet with tears, for the beauty and the glory and the insidious danger of that intoxicating war-cry ; for the blindness and the wickedness and the selfish greed that lurk behind it, exploiting the generous emotions of the young and brave ; for the irony and bitter fatuity of *any* war-cry in a world that should be purged of war.

.   .   .   .   .   .

And so I came to Palmanova to supervise the loading of shell, in the company of Captain Shield and another Ordnance officer.   Shield had travelled much and mixed with Italians on the borders of Abyssinia. He told me that with no other European race were our relations in remote frontier lands more harmonious. They and we have, he said, a perfect code of written and unwritten rules to prevent all friction.   He told me, too, of a young Englishman out there, quite an unimportant person, who had a bad attack of sun-stroke and whose life was in great danger.   The only hope was to get him through quickly to the coast, and the shortest road lay through Italian territory. So application was made to the Italian authorities for a right of passage, which they not only granted, but mapped out his route for him, for it was difficult country and unfamiliar to our people, and sent a guide, and had a mule with a load of ice waiting for him at every halting-place along the road, and so saved his life, treating him with as much consideration and tenderness as they could have been expected to show to a member of their own Royal Family.

.   .   .   .   .   .

Palmanova lies just within the old Italian frontier, a little white town surrounded by a moat, which in summer is quite dry, and by grassy ramparts shaped

like a star. It was first fortified by the Venetian
Republic four hundred years ago, and again by
Napoleon. It can be entered only through one of
three gates, approached by bridges across the moat,
from the north, south-east and south,—the Udine
Gate, the Gradisca Gate and the Maritime Gate.
Each gate is double, so that you pass through a
small square court, almost like a well, and at each
gate you can see the remains of an old portcullis and
drawbridge. Each is topped by two slender towers,
and is wide enough to allow only one vehicle to pass
at a time, and at each there is a guard of Carabinieri
in their grey lantern-hats, to stop and examine all
questionable traffic.

From the ramparts you can see the Carnic and
the Julian Alps, sweeping round the Venetian plain
in a great half circle. To the north the mountains
seem to rise sheer out of green orchards and maize
fields, but to the east there is a gradual slope of less
fertile uplands, where the Austrians in the first days
of war on this Front would not face the onrush of
the Italians in the open, but fell back hurriedly to
the more difficult country behind. At night all the
inhabitants sit out on the ramparts, talking of the
hot weather and the war, and watching the searchlights winking on the hills.

In the centre of the town is a large Piazza, planted
round with myrtles which smell strong and sweet
in the sun, and at midday an old woman sets up a
stall here and sells the newspapers of Rome and Milan,
Bologna and Venetia. In one corner of this Piazza
is a restaurant, where one can play billiards and dine
well and cheaply. A youth serves here who has

been rejected for the Army because of defective
eyesight. He speaks a little French and a little
German and a very little English, and in moments
of excitement words from all these languages come
tumbling out together, mixed up with Italian. He
has, I am sure, an Italian-English phrase book, which
he consults hurriedly in the kitchen, for, whenever
he sets a new course before one, he shoots out
some carefully prepared and usually quite irrelevant
sentence, and watches eagerly to see if one under-
stands. In another corner of the Piazza stands a
campanile with a peal of those absurd little jangling
bells, which are among the most characteristic charms
of Italy. Down a side street is the Albergo Rosa
d'Oro, where for a week I was billeted. The padrone,
a little round man, is always smiling. He thinks the
war will last three years more and seems pleased at
the prospect, for the town and the district round are
full of soldiers, and he must be making great profits.
But his wife, when one speaks of the war, says " it
must end soon ; we must go on hoping that it will
end soon."

The station, where my fatigue party worked, lies
outside the town. When the Austrians provoked
war in 1914, they had special trains waiting here to
carry away the Italian troops who, they hoped, would
go and fight for them against the Russians,—a poor
fool's dream ! In normal times it must be a quiet
place with little traffic. But now there is continual
movement, Infantry going up to the front line and
often waiting for hours at the station, and other
Infantry coming back to rest, goods trains of enormous
length passing through, motor lorries loading and

discharging, driven very skilfully though sometimes very recklessly, horse and mule transport in great variety, both military and civilian, some of the horses wearing straw hats with two holes for the ears, and carts drawn by stolid, slow-moving oxen. With all this coming and going, and with a temperature of over a hundred degrees in the shade, the Albergo della Stazione does a great trade in iced drinks!

I made the acquaintance of two families in this town. At Signor Lazzari's any British officer was always welcome after dinner for music and talk and light refreshments. An Italian General was billeted there and two or three Italian officers of junior rank. A Corporal with a magnificent voice, an operatic singer before the war, came in to sing one night, and a Private from his Battalion played his accompaniment. In Italy, as in France, the art of conversation and a keen joy in it, are still alive, perhaps because Bridge is still almost unknown. Signor Lazzari's handsome and charming daughter was an admirable hostess.

At Signor Burini's I was also most hospitably received and drank some very excellent champagne. I used to talk to his three little girls in the evenings on the ramparts. Signor Burini's mother remembered Garibaldi's visit to Palmanova in 1867, the year after Venetia was liberated from the Austrian yoke and added to United Italy. She was speaking of this one evening to Shield and he said, " It rained very heavily that day, didn't it ? " Whereat the old lady, much astonished and evidently suspecting him of some uncanny gift of second sight, replied that indeed it did. But the truth was that he had

been reading an account of this historic occasion in
a local guide book, which related that, just as Garibaldi came out on a balcony to address the crowd,
a heavy thunderstorm broke and the Hero of the
Two Worlds only said, " You had all better go home
out of the rain."

It can still rain at Palmanova.

One day while I was there the temperature rose
to 105 degrees in the shade, but in the evening a
cool breeze stirred the dust and I sat outside the
Albergo Rosa d'Oro, talking with various passers-by.
About nine o'clock bright lightning began to fill the
sky, but, as yet, no rain.   And then about eleven,
just after I had gone to bed, came a tremendous
drenching thunderstorm and a great whirlwind.
And then, very suddenly, all became quiet again,
save for the rain-water pouring off the roofs into the
street below.

CHAPTER VI

AQUILEIA AND GRADO

ON July 22nd, the day before I returned from
Palmanova to my Battery, Shield and I and
two lorryloads of men made an expedition
in the afternoon to Aquileia and Grado.   Aquileia,
at the height of the old Roman power, was a great
and important city, on the main road eastwards
from the North Italian plain.   It was destroyed and
sacked by Attila and his Huns in the year 452, and

again in 568 by Alboin and his Lombards. It was the
fugitives from Aquileia and the neighbouring towns,
who, taking refuge in the lagoons along the coast,
founded upon certain mudbanks in the fifth century
the city which was destined to be Venice. And it
was at Grado in the year 466 that the foundations
of Venetian constitutional history were laid by the
election of tribunes to govern the affairs of the com-
munity inhabiting the lagoons.

The two chief features of Aquileia to-day are a
museum of Roman antiquities, which I had not time
to visit, and a large church, with a bare interior, but
with a magnificent eleventh century mosaic floor,
one of the best examples of its kind in Italy. The
interior of the church was decorated with flowers
in shell cases, to signify its reconquest by the Italians,
who intend to make here a great national memorial
when the war is over. Beside the church, at its
eastern end, stood a glorious group of very tall
cypresses, one of the best groups I have ever seen,
and opposite the western entrance was a charming
little avenue of young cypresses, planted since the
reconquest. We stayed for half an hour at Aquileia
and then went on to Grado.

.   .   .   .   .   .

On the way Shield told me the story of how the
British Batteries came to Italy. Our own War
Office, as the habit of the tribe is, had wrapped the
whole thing up in mystery, and the Batteries were
christened " the British Mission " to a destination
secret and unnamed. Passing through the South
of France and up the Arc Valley to the frontier, with
the gunners sitting on their guns in open trucks in

the sunshine, the trains were loudly cheered by the French who, in that part of the country, had seen few of the sights of war. Once in Italy the official attempts at mystification mystified nobody. The engine-drivers at Modane hoisted Union Jacks on their engines and kept them flying all the way. Everyone knew who we were and where we were going, and at every station where the trains stopped there were official welcomes and immense crowds cheering like mad. At Turin our guns were wreathed in flowers and at Verona the station staff presented a bouquet to the General, on whose behalf Shield made a suitable reply in Italian.

·   ·   ·   ·   ·   ·

Grado lies on several islands, in its own lagoons. The Austrians were developing it, in a haphazard way, as a watering-place before the war, and there are several large hotels and the beginnings of a Sea Front. The canals are filled with fishing boats with brown sails, which seldom put to sea now for fear of mines.

One approaches Grado by a steamer which starts from a little cluster of houses on the mainland known as Belvedere, and takes one down a long channel through a maze of wooded islands, one of which is now the Headquarters of an Italian Seaplane Squadron. The islands are thickly clothed with tamarisks and pollarded acacias and stone pines, and are reputed to be somewhat malarial. There is a long beach at Grado, where all the world bathes, and the water is deliciously warm, with a bottom of hard sand. Lying in the water, I could see right round the Gulf of Trieste as far as Capodistria, and

straight opposite to me lay Trieste, the Unredeemed
City of Italy's Desire, very clear against a background
of hills. Through glasses I could even distinguish
the trams running in her streets. I could easily
fancy her scarcely a mile away across that sheet of
blue sunlit sea. Thus must she often have appeared
to Italians fighting and dying by sea and land to
reach her, who remained ever just out of reach.

CHAPTER VII

A GRAMOPHONE AND A CHAPLAIN ON THE CARSO

THE Battery moved up to its new position
on the edge of the Carso on the night of
July 25th. The guns were drawn by Italian
tractors. It was a long business getting the guns
out of their gun pits, as we had not much room for
turning, and a still longer one getting them into the
new pits, after unhooking the tractors, down a steep
slope and round two right-angle turns. Owing to
our nearness to the front line no lights could be used
and the night was darker than usual. For hours the
gun detachments were at work with drag ropes,
lowering, guiding and hauling, and the monotonous
cry, that every Siege Gunner knows so well, " On
the ropes—together—heave ! " went echoing round
those rocks till 2 a.m. next morning.

This new position of ours was only three hundred
yards from the Austrians, though we had between

us and them the river Vippacco and a high hill,
a spur of that on which the ruined monastery of
S. Grado di Merna stood. The trenches here ran on
either side of the Vippacco. An Italian Trench
Mortar Battery had been here before us and, it was
said, had been shelled out. But our gun pits, blasted
out of the hillside, were almost completely protected
against hostile fire, except perhaps from guns on
S. Marco, which might, with a combination of good
luck and good shooting, have got us in enfilade.
Only howitzers capable of employing high-angle
fire could usefully occupy such a position, and, as
it was, our shells could not clear the crest except at
pretty large elevations. It resulted that we could
not hit any targets within a considerable distance of
the Austrian front line, but this, we were told, did
not matter. We were here, we were informed, " for
a special purpose " and for action against distant
targets only. There was an orchard on the flat just
behind our guns, a little oasis of fertility in that
barren land, and wooden crosses marking the graves
of some of the Italian Trench Mortar Gunners, who
had preceded us.

Italian Field Artillery were in position all around
us, and were firing a good deal by night. For the
first few nights, with their guns popping off all round,
and with blasting operations in full swing, an almost
continuous echo travelled round and round the stony
hillsides and made me dream that I was sleeping
beside a stormy sea breaking in endless waves on a
rocky coast. Blasting was going on all day and all
night in this neighbourhood. One of our officers
was walking one morning on the back of the Carso,

out of view of the enemy and anticipating no danger,
save the stray shell which is always and everywhere
a possibility in the war zone, when suddenly the face
of an Italian bobbed up from behind a rock with the
warning, in English, " Now shoots the mine ! " and
disappeared again. The Englishman ran for his
life and took shelter behind the same rock, and a
few seconds later there was a heavy explosion, filling
the air with flying fragments, unpleasantly jagged.

Our officers' Mess and sleeping huts were about
two hundred yards from the guns and a little higher
up the hill, just above one of the magnificent newly-
made Italian war roads, along which supplies went
up to Hills 123 and 126 and the Volconiac and Dosso
Faiti. Just outside our huts and opening on to the
road was a broad, natural terrace, with a fine view
backwards over the plain. Several times, during
our first week in this position, the Austrians shelled
a British Battery at Rupa about a mile in rear of
us and an Italian Battery alongside it. It was very
hot and dry and they had been given away by the
huge clouds of dust raised by the blast of their guns
firing. The Austrians shelled them with twelve-
inch and nine-four-fives, getting magnificent shell
bursts, which some of us photographed, great columns
of brown-black smoke, rising mountains high, in the
shape of Prince of Wales' feathers, and hanging for
about ten minutes in the still air. But very little
damage was done, and after a short interval both
Batteries opened fire again.

From this terrace of ours we had fine views of
fighting in the air. On August 2nd we saw an Austrian
plane brought down by two Italians, who dived down

upon him from above, firing at him with machine guns as they swept past him. The Austrian, who was flying high, gradually seemed to lose his head and hesitate in what direction to fly, then he began to turn over and over, recovered for a moment, but finally lost all control and came down nose first into. his own trenches, just across the river. Another evening, about ten o'clock, a whole squadron of Austrian planes came over, flying in regular formation and signalling to one another with Morse lamps. They were going, it appeared, to bomb Gradisca. They were heavily shelled by the " archies " as they came over us, and several fragments of shell fell on our terrace. The night sky was full of starry shell-bursts, and a dozen of our searchlights fussily got busy. Then suddenly all our artillery, as it seemed, began to go off, and for about five minutes there was a deafening burst of fire from guns of all calibres. And then all grew suddenly quiet again. Perhaps it was a raid, perhaps only the fear of one.

One day an Italian plane dropped some booklets into the Austrian trenches, and some were blown back into our own lines. They contained photographs of Austrian prisoners of war in Italian camps, very contented apparently, and explanations in German, Magyar and various Slav tongues, showing " men who yesterday were living from hour to hour in peril of death, now waiting happily and calmly in perfect safety for the war to end, when they shall return to their homes to embrace once more their wives and little children. Here you will be able to recognise many of your friends." A good propaganda to induce desertions and surrenders ! The Italians generally had the mastery over the Austrians in the air. Their machines, and especially their Capronis, could always be distinguished from the Austrians' by the deeper hum of their engines.

Venosta had a gramophone, which played most evenings after dinner on the terrace, chiefly marches and martial music and Italian opera. Italy's Libyan war, whatever else may be said of it, has produced one magnificent marching song, " A Tripoli," which deserves to live for ever. Fine, too, even on the gramophone, are the " March of the Alpini," the " March of the Bersaglieri " and the famous " Garibaldi's Hymn." I met an English doctor once, who had heard this last played in Rome on some great occasion with some of the old Garibaldian veterans in their red shirts marching in front of the band. He had felt a lump in his throat that day, he said. When Venosta's gramophone played, the Italians encamped near by clustered round the edge of the terrace in obvious enjoyment, and sometimes one or two would dash indignantly down the road to stop limbers and carts, which were making a rattle on the stones.

.   .   .   .   .   .

Our Mess was a great centre for visitors, both English and Italian, we being at this time the British Battery in the most advanced and interesting position. Among our visitors, especially on Sundays, was a Chaplain, whom I will call Littleton, who used to conduct our Church Parades. In the British Army, and I believe in most others, the principle of compulsory religious observance is still intermittently enforced, when it does not interfere with the still more important business of fighting. I liked Littleton very much in many ways, but sometimes he infuriated me. He was lunching with us one day and describing how for some months in France, during some murderous fighting, he was attached to an Infantry Battalion. " I have never in my life enjoyed myself more," he said, "than during those months." I could not help asking, " What did you enjoy, seeing the poor devils getting hit ? " I told him afterwards that I knew he did not really delight in spectacles of agony and bloodshed, but that " enjoy " seemed to me an unfortunate word to use.

On another occasion I attended, in the capacity of Orderly Officer for the day, one of Littleton's Church Parades and heard him preach. It was clear that he was troubled by a suspicion that the war and the details of its development had discredited in some minds some of the ideas of which he was the professional exponent. He made a brave struggle, however, against this tide of unreason. " God does not make things too easy for us," he explained, " He gives us the opportunities, and if we choose not to use them, that is our fault. A loving father sets up a tremendously high standard for his son, and judges him severely, not in spite of, but because of, his love for him. In God's sight, three or four years of war may be tremendously worth while."

Then we sang a hymn. I felt inclined to sing instead a song, written by a soldier who was wounded in France :—

> " The Bishop tells us, ' when the boys come back
> They will not be the same ; for they'll have fought

In a just cause : they led the last attack
On Anti-Christ ; their comrades' blood has bought
New right to breed an honourable race.
They have challenged Death and dared him face to face.'
' We're none of us the same ! ' the boys reply.
For George lost both his legs ; and Bill's stone blind ;
Poor Jim's shot through the lungs and like to die ;
And Bert's gone syphilitic ; you'll not find
A chap who served there hasn't found *some* change.'
And the Bishop said ' The ways of God are strange ! ' "

It was hard for such a limited intelligence as mine,
especially in this unending Italian sunshine, to imagine
that it could seriously be worth while to burn down
a whole real world, in order to roast a probably
imaginary pig. I found it very hard to believe,
with the Chaplains, that the war was purifying everyone's character, and I was particularly sceptical as
regards some of the elderly non-combatants who were
unable to realise at first hand " the Glory of the Great
Adventure."

CHAPTER VIII

A FRONT LINE RECONNAISSANCE

EVERY day, in our Group, some officer carried
out a Front Line Reconnaissance. This officer
was chosen in rotation from the Group Headquarters and the various Batteries. Colonel Raven,
our Group Commander, often carried out these Reconnaissances himself. Of all British officers at this
time serving in Italy, he had, I think, the greatest
understanding of the Italians. He had travelled

4

in Italy in peace-time and had studied Italian history.
He fully appreciated the difficulties against which
the Italian Army had to contend, and its military
achievements in spite of them. He enjoyed social
intercourse with Italians, and his invariable and
slightly elaborate courtesy was, in an Englishman,
remarkable. For, as Mazzini once said, an Englishman's friendship, when once secured, holds very
firm, but it is manifested more by deeds than by
words. But Colonel Raven had the gift of sympa-
thetic imagination, and he had also in full measure
the Allied spirit.

The purpose of these Reconnaissances was twofold :
first, to report on matters of military importance,
any notable activity by the enemy, the direction and
nature of hostile fire upon our trenches, the effects of
our own fire, when not otherwise ascertainable, the
precise position on the map, especially after any
action, of our own and of the enemy's lines, including
saps, advanced posts and the like ; second, to maintain
a real contact and spirit of comradeship with the
Italian Infantry and to seek to give them confidence
in the efficiency and promptitude of British Artillery
support. Under the first head, valuable information
was frequently brought back, and under the second
I believe that, so far at least as our Group was concerned, the personal relations between the Artillery
and the Infantry were exceptionally good. Hardly
ever did we receive complaints that our guns were
firing short, though such complaints are often made,
and often quite groundlessly, when the Infantry
lack confidence in the Artillery behind them.

.   .   .   .   .   .

At one time thin-skinned persons among us used to complain that Italians who passed them on the roads used to call out " imboscato ! " Imboscato is a term very frankly used in the Italian army, generally though not necessarily as a term of reproach. It corresponds with the French " embusqué," one who shelters in a wood, for which we in English have no precise equivalent. It is used by an Italian to indicate one who runs, or is thought to run, less risk of death than the speaker. It is chiefly used of men in the non-combatant services or in posts well behind the fighting front, including the Higher Staff and especially the junior ranks attendant on them. It is used also in jest by Italian patrols going out at night into No Man's Land, of their comrades, whom they leave behind in the front line trenches. Personally I was never called an imboscato, nor were any of my brother gunners, except once or twice when riding in side-cars or motors miles in rear of our guns. And to Infantry marching along dusty roads under an Italian sun there is something very irritating in a motor car dashing past, with its occupants reclining in easy positions, its siren hideously shrieking, and blinding dust-clouds rising in its wake.

German propaganda was insidiously active in Italy throughout the war, and spread many lying stories with the object of discrediting the British. Among these was one, the details of which do not matter now, concerning the fact that only British Artillery, and no British Infantry, had at that time been sent to Italy. Our Reconnaissances, involving our visible and daily presence among the gallant succession of Italian Brigades, who held the blood-

stained line on the Carso and across the valley of
the Vippacco, were the most fitting reply which we
could make to German propaganda.

.   .   .   .   .   .

I made my first Front Line Reconnaissance on
July 27th, two days after we had moved forward to
our new Battery position. That day I visited the
trenches on the Volconiac, starting in the early afternoon and getting back at nightfall. I took with me
as a guide a young Italian gunner, a Neapolitan by
birth, who had been a waiter in an Italian restaurant
in New York before the war. He had been in the
Austrian offensive of 1916 in the Trentino, where
all the guns of his Battery had been lost and nearly
all his comrades killed or captured.

From the Battery position we followed the road
behind Hill 123, up a glorious valley, whose sides
were thickly wooded with pines, gradually thinning
under the destruction wrought by Austrian shell fire
and the Italian military need for timber. The only
other vegetation here was a little coarse grass. On
the lee side of Hill 123, sheltered from Austrian fire,
was a whole village of wooden huts, admirably constructed, capable of housing several Battalions. At
the head of the valley, the road, a good example
of the war work of the Italian Engineers, turned
sharply up the hillside, securing tolerable gradients
by means of constant zigzags—tolerable that is to
say for men on foot and for pack mules, for wheeled
transport could not proceed beyond this point. It
was a steep climb and I perspired most visibly right
through my thin tunic. Three-quarters of the way

up we stopped and got a drink of water from the Infantrymen in charge of the water barrels. There are no springs or streams on the Volconiac or on Dosso Faiti. All water has to be pumped up from below through pipes, and at the point where we rested, water barrels were being continually filled from the pipes and then hauled on by hand, on sleighs, for the remainder of the ascent. Water was also carried up from this point by individual soldiers in the fiaschi, or glass bottles encased in plaited straw, in which Italian wine is sold.

Just below the crest we entered the trenches, which were held at this time by the Florence Brigade. The construction of these trenches was very interesting. They were all blasted in the rock, and many drilling machines were at work as I passed along them, increasing the number of *caverne*, or dug-outs, and deepening those already in existence. Here and there, where the trenches were rather shallow, they were built up with loose rocks and sandbags filled with stones.

One of my objects was to get a view of the Austrian trenches and barbed wire on the Tamburo, in order to observe from closer quarters than was possible from any of our O.P.'s the effects of our recent bombardments, and to verify or disprove a report that certain new defensive works were being constructed by the enemy at night. Our own trenches here were on a higher level than the enemy's, and the bottom of the valley between the Tamburo and this part of the Volconiac was in No Man's Land, as was a relatively short slope on the Tamburo and a relatively long slope on the Volconiac. The latter slope was very steep, but thickly clothed with pines, most of which were now shattered by shell fire into mere dead stumps. Even these stumps, however, made it difficult to get an uninterrupted view of the Tamburo, and I had to go some miles along the trenches, gazing through numerous peepholes, before I reached a point from which I could satisfy myself that our bombardments had been effective and that the reported new works were indeed real. Having got this information, I smoked a pipe and talked with an Italian company commander in a rocky dug-out, and then started to return.

Things were quiet on this sector of the Front that afternoon, though Italian Field Guns were bursting shrapnel from time to time over the Tamburo. As I went along the trenches I was several times greeted by Italians who had been in America, " Hullo, John ! How are you ?   How d'you like this dam country ? " This type brings back with it across the Atlantic the frank, almost brutal, familiarity of a new and demo-cratic civilisation.   It contrasts oddly with the quieter ways of those Italians who have lived all their lives in Italy, amid one of the oldest and most mature civilisations of the world.

On our way down the hill we passed a seemingly endless string of pack mules coming up, laden with food and ammunition. Always at evening this wonderful system of supply was visibly working, triumphing over tremendous natural difficulties. We passed, too, a party of about fifty men hauling up on long ropes a heavy drilling engine, the sort of labour of which British fatigue parties have, luckily for themselves, no experience. Mists came down from the mountains as we descended, and rainstorms threatened, but did not break.

CHAPTER IX

AN EVENING AT GORIZIA

ON the first day in August I had been doing some observation at S. Andrea in the afternoon, and, this duty over, I got permission to walk into Gorizia and visit the section of the British Red Cross stationed there, several of whose members I knew. It is a longer walk than one would think, for S. Andrea is practically a southern suburb of Gorizia, which, however, straggles over a large area of country. The railway bridge across the Isonzo is broken down by shell fire and so are two other bridges,—all three of stone,—but these could be soon repaired, if we made a big advance. It would be wasted labour to repair them now, for the Austrians would only break them down again. The Italians have run up a low, broad wooden bridge, sheltered from Austrian view behind one of the broken stone bridges. From time to time the Austrians hit this bridge, and then the Italians quickly make it good again. To be able to cross the Isonzo at this point is a convenience, but not a military necessity, for all movement of troops and supplies into Gorizia can be carried out on the left bank of the river and across bridges some miles further down-stream.

The suburbs of the town were badly knocked about, but the centre was not at this time much damaged.

Gorizia lies in a salient of the hills, with the Austrians looking down upon it from the tops of most of them. But, still hoping to win it back, they do not shell it heavily or often. There are special reasons, too, for their forbearance. For Gorizia is a sort of Austrian Cheltenham, whither Austrian officers retire in large numbers to pass their last years in villas which they take over from one another's widows. So the Austrian officer class has a sort of vested interest in the preservation of the place. So also have certain Hebrew Banks in Vienna, which hold mortgages on a great part of the land in and around the city, which just before the war was being rapidly developed as a fashionable Spa. It is a well laid out town, with large public gardens and good buildings, architecturally very like the larger Italian towns on the other side of the old frontier, Udine for example, but with a certain element of a heavier and more *rococo* style, the Viennese. There is still a fairly large civilian population in the town, and one restaurant still keeps open.

I found the British Red Cross in the Via Ponte Isonzo, in what had once been a big boarding-house, with a large untidy garden behind. Most of those stationed there were motor ambulance drivers, about twenty in number, some too old to fight, some rejected for health, some Quakers, unwilling to kill, but willing to risk their own lives on behalf of the wounded, others again boys under military age, who go, as soon as they can, to the Navy or the Flying Corps. It is brave and nervous work they do, driving ambulances in the dark, without lights and under fire.

RAILWAY BRIDGE OVER THE ISONZO WRECKED BY AUSTRIAN SHELLFIRE. VIEW LOOKING WESTWARD FROM GORIZIA. ON THE LEFT WOODEN BRIDGE BUILT BY ITALIAN ENGINEERS

After dinner I sat out in the garden in the twilight and talked with an old acquaintance of mine, who has had a large share in the organisation and daily work of the British Red Cross in Italy.   The Italians, he said, are really beginning to feel their feet, as a united nation, in this war.   Men of all classes from all parts of Italy are meeting and mixing with one another as they have never done before, and the old *regionalismo* is being rapidly undermined.   He himself has almost ceased to think critically of the past or speculatively of the future, but just lives and works in the present.   As to the state of the world after the war, he is very confident, provided we go on fighting long enough.   Nothing that happens at home is of great importance, all the pressure is on the Fronts.   Everything is looking now in the direction of democracy.   Even Russia, in the long run unconquerable, has got her good out of the war already, whatever miseries and transitory anarchy she may have yet to undergo.   In England and elsewhere many of the present political leaders are vile, but we shall all know what we want the world to look like, and to *be* like, after the war, and new leaders will arise and lead us.   When the survivors of our smitten generation have grown old, there must be a peace of hearts, as well as a peace of arms, between the young of all lands.   But our generation can never make personal friendships again with Germans, seeing that they have killed nearly all those who mattered most to us, and that we have to spend the rest of our lives without them.

He motored me back to the Vippacco bridge at

Rubbia. When next I heard of him it was a month later at the height of the Italian offensive. He had been severely wounded on the Bainsizza Plateau.

The British Red Cross did splendid work in Italy and made a big contribution to Anglo-Italian friendship and understanding. They began their operations in Italy in September 1915, and were thus the first Englishmen to "show the flag" on the Italian Front. Thousands of Italians will gratefully and affectionately remember them till the end of their lives. More even than the British fighting troops who came after them, the British Red Cross will remain a historic legend in Italy in the days to come.

CHAPTER X

A CEMETERY AT VERSA

I WAS at Versa, as I have already said, from the 2nd to the 10th of August, to supervise a party working on the hospital. I walked one evening down the village street, where in the light of the sunset an Italian military band was playing to a mixed crowd of soldiers and civilians. Just outside the village I came to the gates of a cemetery, where six tall cypresses stand like sentinels on guard over the graves of many hundreds of Italian dead. This was at first a civilian graveyard, but all the dead have Italian names, except one Kirschner, and even he was called Giuseppe and has an Italian inscription on his tombstone. For this is Italia Redenta, in this one little corner of which a great company of Italian youth have already laid down their lives. And now the graves, in long straight rows, have filled one newly added field, and begun to flow across a second, and soon from the Field Hospitals in the village more dead will come.

Here, as in our war graveyards in France, no religious dogma or supernatural hope intrudes upon the little wooden crosses. On these, for the most part, you can read only the bare conventional attributes of each little handful of dust, which has passed through its quivering agony into the still sleep of decay,—its name and regiment, its civilian home, the place and date of its death. A few have more than this. Here lie the two brothers Bellina in one grave, with a cross at their head and another, rougher and larger, at their feet, announcing simply, " I due fratelli," " the two brothers." And here is a tombstone engraved with an anchor, for one who, very early in the war, was hit while fording the Isonzo in face of the enemy's fire. " Al Pontiere Guazzaro Giuseppe che valorosamente sfidando le infide acque dell' Isonzo cadeva colpito dal piombo nemico. 25 Giugno 1915." [1] And here is another inscription, typical of that Latin sense of comradeship, which is more articulate, though not necessarily more profound, than ours. " Sottotenente Arcangeli Antonio, con commossa memoria," the officers of his Battery, " il loro orgoglio infinito quì eternano." " In deeply moved remembrance they here place

[1] " To the Sapper Giuseppe Guazzaro, who fell, while bravely defying the treacherous waters of the Isonzo, struck down by an enemy bullet, 25th June, 1915."

upon eternal record their infinite pride in him." It is poor stuff in English, but a vivid and quite natural tribute in Italian.

.   .   .   .

Where the sun went down, the sky was a sea of rose red and golden green, studded with little long islands of dark cloud, and on the edge of this sea the evening star twinkled like a tiny illumined boat, dancing, a blaze of light, upon the waves. To left and right the cloudbanks were a deep purple blue, fast fading into the dim warm grey of an Italian night. East and north the mountains that bound the plain, silent witnesses of Italy's great struggle, were hidden in the dusk, and the cypress sentinels stood up sharp and black against the darkening sky. The band had ceased to play and one heard only the chirp of grasshoppers, and across an orchard the soft sound of Italian speech, and the distant song of two soldiers in the village street. But the warm air, which just now was throbbing with a military march, seemed to be throbbing still with an aching longing that happier days may come swiftly to this land of beauty and pain, so that the sacrifice of all these dead shall not be wholly waste.

.   .   .   .   .   .

Not many miles away, as the sun was setting, an Austrian shell burst in a British Battery, and three hours later through the dark under faint stars an ambulance lorry brought to us the bodies of four British gunners, whose dust will mingle with Italian dust, under Italian skies, for ever.

CHAPTER XI

UDINE

I FIRST saw Udine on the 5th of August. I was still on duty at Versa, but the conversation in the R.A.M.C. Mess bored me, particularly at meals ; it was all sputum and latrines, gas gangrene and the relative seniority of the doctors one to another. There was nothing to keep me at Versa, for my gunner fatigue party did not in truth need any supervision. So I determined to go to Udine. I started, walking, about 10 a.m. It was not too hot. I walked about three miles and then picked up a lorry. One can generally get a ride on an Italian lorry if there is any room, by waving one's stick at the driver, shouting out one's destination, and looking agreeable. This one took me to Mogaredo and then stopped. I then walked another three miles to a point near Trevignano. Here I was within ten miles of Udine and picked up another lorry which took me the rest of the way. It was driven by a Triestino who, seeing what was coming, had left the Unredeemed City just before Italy declared war. His face was very sad, and he made a gesture of weeping, drawing his fingers downwards from his eyes across his cheeks, though his eyes were dry. " How long ? " he asked. " How long before Trieste will be free ? "

We approached Udine through a long avenue of plane trees, planted under Napoleon. It is a gay little town, with arcaded streets, clustering round a hill on the top of which stands a Castello, with a memorial tower to the martyrs of 1848, and on the hill slopes public gardens full of cypresses. Udine was at this time a nest of British newspaper correspondents. I began to make their acquaintance in the afternoon. First an Anglo-Italian lady from Rome, whom I met sitting out behind the Hôtel Grande d'Italia under the shade of trees. She was evidently something of a figure here and received several callers, all ladies of Udine, as we sat drinking coffee. One of these, on learning that I was a gunner, took out a locket and handed it to me. It contained a picture of a marvellously handsome boy. It was her eldest son, killed three months before in Cadore, a Lieutenant in a Mountain Battery. He was only nineteen. His mother began to weep as she handed me the locket, and it was the lady from Rome who told me these things. Then the mother cried, between her sobs, " E troppo crudele, la guerra ! " And as I handed the locket back, I thought of the unmarried childless parson in khaki who considered that " three or four years of war may be tremendously worth while."

.   .   .   .   .   .

Later I met and dined with two of the male correspondents of the London Press. Conversation, in the sense of a mere flow of talk, is never difficult with newspaper men. They are among the most articulate of the British, although much that they articulate is only patter. These two had plenty of miscellaneous information, much of which I received in a sceptical spirit, but I learned some interesting facts, which I verified from other sources later on. Chief of these

was the effect produced upon Young Italy by the
personal gallantry of the poet D'Annunzio, who,
when he is not flying at the head of the Italian bombing planes against Pola, is making fiery orations to
the Infantry in the front line and distributing
among them little tricolor flags bearing his own
autograph.

Having talked till midnight, I found a bedroom
at the Croce Malta, where I slept for four hours.   Then
I got up and dressed and walked to the railway
station, where I drank coffee and ate biscuits.   A
train was due to leave for Palmanova, the nearest
station to Versa, at 5.30 a.m.   As I waited for it on
the platform, I looked out at the station lights, a
dull orange under their dark shades, and at the red
signals beyond, four in a vertical line, and beyond
again at the dim outlines of houses and dark trees
against a sky, at first a very deep dark blue, but slowly
lighting up with the beginning of the dawn. The
train did not start till nearly seven. By this time
it was quite light, and the sun had turned the
distant Cadore into a ridge of pink grey marble,
very sharply outlined against the morning sky, and
in the middle distance, just across the maize fields
which run beside the railway track, rose the *campanile*
of some little village of Friuli, like a stick of shining
alabaster.

CHAPTER XII

THE BRITISH AND THE ITALIAN SOLDIER

THE sending of ten British Batteries to Italy had something more than a military significance. Otherwise the thing was hardly worth doing. It was evident that here was an international gesture. An effort was being made to promote a real Anglo-Italian understanding, to substitute for those misty and unreal personifications—" England " to an Italian, " Italy " to an Englishman—real personal knowledge and a sense of individual comradeship in a great cause. Our task, in short, was not only to fight, but also to fraternise. But would we fraternise successfully? For it has been said, not without some truth, that " England is an island and every Englishman is an island," and in the early days I was doubtful what sort of personal effect we should produce, and what sort of personal impressions our men would bring away.

When I got back to the Battery from Versa I began to take stock of my own impressions so far, and to notice, in the letters which I had to censor, the drift of general opinion. It was surprisingly satisfactory.

" Some of these Italians," writes one gunner, " are the finest fellows you could wish to meet. Our men get on very well with them." " The Italians," writes another, " are very good soldiers ánd nice chaps. We get on well together." " The other night," writes a third, " I was out laying telephone wires in a grave-yard. We saw some Italian soldiers carrying a tombstone for their Lieutenant who had recently been killed. The Italians look after their graves very well. A Sergeant, who had spent most of his life in England, asked us in and gave us some coffee and cognac which was jolly acceptable. He asked if we had any old English papers, as he was forgetting all his English, as he had been away from England for five years.''   And a fourth writes, " The great majority of these Italians have been in different parts of America " (this of course is a wild exaggeration !), " they are very delighted to have a chat. In fact I think the Italian people are very sociable. Nearly all the boys can begin to make themselves understood." These tributes are obviously sincere. They occur in the midst of good-natured grumbles about the heat, and the monotony of macaroni and rice and stew, and of requests for " more fags " and of hopes that " this business will soon be over."

The fact that so many Italians, having lived in England and America, can speak English and know something of us and our ways, accounts for much. For a foreign language is the Great Barrier Reef against the voyages of ordinary people towards international understanding. And the country counts for something, too. Its natural obstacles compel admiration for an Army which has achieved so much in spite of them. And I am sure that no British gunner, however inarticulate, who has served in Italy, and especially those young fellows who, when war broke out, stood only on the threshold of their manhood, with their minds still wide open for new impressions, has not felt some sort of secret thrill at the astounding and incomparable beauty of this country, the very

5

contemplation of which sometimes brings one near
to weeping.

I recall, for instance, a tough old Sergeant Major,
with twenty-seven years' service with our Artillery
all over the world, an utterly unromantic person.
He and I were bringing back my working party on
the 10th of August from Versa to Rubbia in a lorry.
The men were singing loudly, and greeted an Italian
sentry on Peteano bridge with cheerful cries of " Buona
sera, Johnny ! " And the Sergeant Major suddenly
observed to me that " this must be a fine country in
peace-time," and went on to praise the mountains,
and the rivers, and the trees, especially the cypresses,
and the surface of the roads, and some town behind
the lines, Udine I think, which was " very pretty "
and " quite all right." The Italians, too, were " all
right," which from him was most high praise. And
then, as though half ashamed of having said so much,
he added, rather hastily, " But there's nothing to
touch the old country after all. I think I shall
settle down there when this war's over. I've had
about enough of foreign parts."

And what do the Italians think of us, I wonder ?
I only know that they treat us always with great
friendliness, and show great interest in our guns and
all our doings. So the international gesture has, I
think, begun already to succeed. And its success
will grow. For those British graves, which we shall
leave behind us—some are dug and filled already—
will tell their own story to the future. They will be
facts, if only tiny facts, both in British and Italian
history, and " far on in summers that we shall not
see," bathed in the warm brilliance of Italian sunshine,

'they will bear witness to Anglo-Italian comradeship
across the years.

CHAPTER XIII

I JOIN THE FIRST BRITISH BATTERY IN ITALY

ON the 15th of August arrived an operation
order indicating our targets in the first and
second phases of the great Italian offensive,
which had been long expected, and also the objectives
of the Infantry. The day on which the offensive
was to begin was not yet announced. Six more
British Siege Batteries, giving us now three British
Heavy Artillery Groups, had arrived on the Carso and
in the Monfalcone sector about a fortnight before.
The French too had sent a number of Heavy Batteries,
which were in position on Monte Sabotino and elsewhere north of the Vippacco. But the counsel of
wise men had been disregarded, and no French or
British Infantry, no complete Allied Army Corps,
had been sent to the Italian Front, where a big military
success could have been more easily obtained and
would have had greater military and political results
at this time, than anywhere else.

On this day I walked to and from S. Andrea, returning to the Battery in the evening greatly perspiring but with an enormous appetite. Large numbers
of Infantry were going up the Vallone and the
Volconiac in the dusk. Italian Infantry march in
twos on either side of a road, not in fours on one side
as ours do.

The Austrians shelled a good deal this evening, and put a lot of gas shell into Merna.

. . . . .

On the 17th I was transferred to another Battery. It was the eve of the offensive, and my new Battery was an officer short, while my old Battery was again at full strength, the officer who had been in hospital wounded, when I arrived in Italy, having now returned. I joined my new Battery about midday. They were in position on the Vippacco, close to the former position of my old Battery. I was destined to stay with them for seventeen months, till after the war was won, and I came to identify myself very completely with them, and to be proud to be one of them.

This had been the first of all the British Batteries to come into action in Italy, and had fired the first British shell against Austria. The Major in command had the reputation of being the most efficient British Battery Commander in Italy, and, so far as my experience of others went, he deserved it. He was a Regular soldier, and had served with a Mountain Battery in India, a service which requires and breeds a power of quick decision, by no means universal among Garrison Gunners of the Regular Army. Personally he was a most delightful man, at his best a very amusing talker, a pleasant companion and an excellent Commanding Officer. Few officers whom I have met took as much thought and trouble as he for the material welfare of his men. From his junior officers he combined a demand for high efficiency with a sometimes wonderful solicitude for their comfort, health and peace of mind. He never asked any of us to do more, or even as much, as he did willingly himself, and if anything went wrong in the Battery, which it seldom did, he never hesitated, in dealing with higher authorities, to take all the blame. He had been twice wounded already, once on the Somme and again in the Italian May offensive. Later on he was wounded a third time.

Captain Jeune, the Second-in-Command, was also a Regular, but very young. In mind and manner he was older than his years, and he knew his work as a military professional extremely well. Some found him truculent, but he never displayed any truculence to me.

On my arrival I became Senior Subaltern of the Battery. The three Junior Subalterns, Darrell, Leary and Winterton, provided a variety of companionship. Darrell was a man of business, a most capable officer, a good Mess Secretary, and very easy to get on with. Leary was a dark-haired Irishman, who had originated in the County Limerick. He was a good mathematician, but in conversation was apt to be long-winded, and had a wonderful capacity for making a simple matter appear complex. He had been, by turns, a civil engineer and an actor, and had a fine singing voice. As an officer he was infinitely laborious and conscientious, but with a queer disconcerting streak of Irish unaccountability. One never quite knew what he would do, if left alone in charge of anything.

Winterton was a good-looking boy, who would have gone up to Cambridge in 1915, if there had been no war. Instead he enlisted in the Horse Artillery, became a Corporal, and went to the Dardanelles as a Despatch Rider. Having spent several months in hospital at Malta and nearly died of dysentery, he came back to England and was given an Artillery Commission. He was a gallant youth but just a little casual, with rather a music-hall mind, but good company, if one was not left alone with him too long.

There was also attached to the Battery at this time an Italian Artillery officer, whom I will call Manzoni, a Southerner, small and very dark. He had taught himself to speak excellent English though he had never been in England. He was an intelligent observer and an amusing companion, and we became great friends.

The personnel of the Battery was splendid, and I do not believe that in any other Battery the spirit of the men was better, nor the personal relations between officers and men on a sounder and healthier footing, than with us.

Some Battery Commanders proceed on the principle that even the most experienced N.C.O. cannot be trusted to perform the simplest duty, except under the eye of an officer, however junior. The Battery in this case becomes helplessly dependent on the officers. If they go out of action, so does the whole Battery. Other Battery Commanders, of whom my new Major was one, proceed on the principle that as many N.C.O.'s as possible should be able to do an officer's work, so that the Battery should be able to continue in action without any officers at all if necessary, and also be able to adapt itself readily to a sudden change from stagnant to open warfare. This principle is universally applied in the French Artillery, where, apart from its evident wisdom, it has been necessitated

ITALIAN MULE TRANSPORT ON THE CARSO

NO. 3 GUN OF THE FIRST BRITISH BATTERY IN ITALY (AT PEC)

by the great shortage of officers. My own Major used to train all our best N.C.O.'s with this object in view and, when satisfied of their competence, used to give them in normal times considerable responsibilities in the working of the Battery in action. The result was that we had as capable and reliable a set of " Numbers One " and " B.C.A.'s " as could be found anywhere.[1] The men thoroughly appreciated the amount of trust reposed in them and never failed us. Furthermore, when I joined the Battery there was hardly a man who was not a trained specialist, either as a Signaller, Gunlayer or B.C.A.

Seventeen months later, only the Major, Leary and myself, out of the officers in the Battery when I joined, still remained with it, and death, wounds, sickness, promotion and commissions from the ranks had taken from us many of our best N.C.O.'s and men. But through all the varied experiences of those long months, there had been a continuity of tradition and an unchanging spirit. We were still, for me and for many, the First British Battery in Italy.

---

[1] A " Number One " is the Sergeant or other N.C.O. in charge of a gun and its detachment when in action. A " B.C.A. " (or Battery Commander's Assistant) assists the officer on duty in the Command Post in locating points on the map, in making numerical calculations, and in other miscellaneous duties.

PART III

THE ITALIAN SUMMER OFFENSIVE, 1917

CHAPTER XIV

THE OFFENSIVE OPENS

ON the 18th of August I got up at half-past four in the morning. There was a mist in the air, which cleared away as the day grew warmer. The big bombardment in what the journalists called the Twelfth Battle of the Isonzo began at six o'clock and went on continuously all day. Once the thing was started, I had little to do except to change occasionally the rate of fire,—" *lento*," " *normale*," " *vivace*," " *celere*" and " *double vivace*" by turns. The first part of the day I was in charge of the Right Section of the Battery and sat most of the time on a wooden bench at a table under a tarpaulin among the acacias. By my side sat a telephonist in communication with the Battery Command Post, some four hundred yards away to the left, beyond the Left Section. My only other apparatus was a megaphone, a notebook and pencil, and a pipe. Occasionally I would go and stand by one of the guns, to check the gun-laying and to see that the guns were recoiling and coming up again without undue violence. One had also to guard against a dust cloud being raised by the blast of the guns, thus giving away our position to the enemy. To prevent this, we formed a chain of men every half hour to pass water-buckets from hand to hand, from the river just behind us down the sunken road, to lay the dust in and around the gun pits. But under an Italian August sun the ground soon grew parched and dusty again.

The Austrians did not shell much till the evening, when they nearly hit our Mess and shell-shocked a man of another Battery in the road close by. But the Italian bombardment all day was very heavy, and our guns and theirs were to go on firing all night. Just before midnight I relieved the Major in the Command Post, and he and the rest of the officers went to bed. So I sat there wakefully among the acacias, awaiting any sudden orders from the Group to switch or lift to new targets, or to vary the rate of fire. Every now and then I took a walk round the Battery to see that all was working correctly, and every hour the N.C.O.'s in charge of each gun brought in their fired tubes to the Command Post and reported how many rounds had been fired in the preceding hour and how many tubes misfired.

.   .   .   .   .   .

It was a clear, starlight night, up above the multitudinous flashes of British and Italian guns. At close quarters these flashes were blindingly bright, and flung up showers of red sparks. In the intervals of a few seconds between flashes, if one stood with one's eyes fixed on the guns, the stars seemed blotted out in an utterly black darkness. A long bombardment is one of the most boring things in the world by reason of its intense monotony, and because in a queer half-unconscious way it begins, after many hours, very slightly to fray the nerves. Listening and watching in the small hours, and from time to time directing, I found myself able, with almost discreditable elastic-mindedness, to call up at will any of the aspects of modern war,—its utter and inherent wickedness, its artistic and scientific majesty, its occasional moral justification against the oppressor, its ultimate blank insanity. But I would not have liked to be an Austrian yesterday or this morning. The Italian Infantry attacked on our sector at 5.30 a.m. There was a tremendous crescendo of gunfire at this time. The Major relieved me in the Command Post at 5 o'clock, and urged me to go to bed, but I did not feel inclined to sleep. Instead I went up about 6 o'clock through Pec village to an O.P. on a hillside beyond, to see what could be seen. But all the Front was hidden in a thick mist, made thicker by the smoke, shot through with innumerable momentary flashes. All round us thousands of guns were going off, filling the air with a deafening and continuous roar. A telephonist was with me who had been through a good deal of the Somme fighting, and had found the Italian Front, in times of lull, a little uneventful. But this morning he was full of appreciation. " This is something like it, isn't it, Sir ? " he said. Being able to see nothing, I went back to bed for some hours and spent the afternoon at a Battery O.P., which had been specially arranged for this offensive, in an Italian reserve trench just off the Pec-Merna road.

.   .   .   .   .   .

The bombardment continued through the 19th

and 20th and 21st of August, now with guns firing independently, now with salvos or rounds of Battery fire,
now with individual guns being ranged afresh from
some O.P., with hardly an hour's interval of silence.
How little the individual soldier knows of what is
happening at these times! Conflicting rumours of
varying credibility came in to us during those three
days, rumours of big advances both to the north and
to the south. But on our own sector we knew that
no permanent advance had been made, for we were
still firing a good deal on old " Zone 15," one of our
first day's targets, and on that damned Hill 464, the
most important of the first objectives of the Infantry.

Before this offensive began I had slept in a hut
above ground, but the Major had now insisted that
I should sleep in a small dug-out half-way up a steep
bank, at the bottom of which our Mess Hut stood
in an orchard stretching down to the river bank.
The Austrians shelled us intermittently, but without
doing any damage. In the small hours of the 21st
I was dozing in my dug-out, where I had been reading
Lowes Dickinson's *Choice Before Us*, a congenial book
at such a time, with nine-tenths of which I was in
complete agreement. I then heard a series of Austrian
" 4.2's " come sailing over my dug-out and burst just
at the foot of the bank. They made miserable bursts
in the soft earth, so small as to make me suspect gas
shells for a moment, but this suspicion did not worry
me, for no one was sleeping at the bottom and gas
cannot run uphill. Next morning I found a shell
hole fifteen yards from the Mess Hut, another on the
path and several others among the trees. They
were " double events," with a shrapnel and time fuse

head and a high explosive and percussion fuse tail, but neither head nor tail had been of much effect. There was very heavy firing that morning, but less in the afternoon. Great gloom prevailed on our sector, where we were back again in most of our first positions. The Infantry were reported to be unable to make headway against machine guns on Hill 464 and the Tamburo. To the south, on the Carso, the ruins of the village of Selo had been taken, but not much else.

But, though we did not know it then, the Italian Army in those first three days had won magnificent successes to the north of us.

CHAPTER XV

WE SWITCH OUR GUNS NORTHWARD

ON the 22nd of August we got for the first time definite news of the Italian advance on the Bainsizza Plateau. The day was rather hotter than usual, and on our own sector there was still no appreciable progress. Hill 464 had been won and lost three times since yesterday morning, and, to the south of it, Hill 368 also had been won and lost again. Up there it must be a vain and shocking shambles. It was claimed for Cadorna's communiqués, I think justly, that at this time no others were more moderate and truthful. No point was claimed as won, until it was not merely won but securely held.

The Italian Battery beside us were moving north that night to the Tolmino sector and next day our Left Section was to move out into a position in the open, in order to switch north and shell S. Marco, which we could not reach from our present gun pits. S. Marco, being north of the Vippacco, was in the area of the Italian Second Army, commanded by Capello, which had been performing the great feats of these last days. It was clear that, for the moment, the main Italian effort was being made to the north.

Indeed by the 24th all the British guns of our Group were pointing north-eastward, firing at S. Marco and neighbouring targets. British casualties and those of the Italian Heavy Artillery had been very light, the Austrian having concentrated practically all his Artillery fire, in addition to his machine guns, on the Italian Infantry, amongst whom there had been hideous slaughter.

But in the early morning of the 23rd an Austrian shell killed a Sergeant and two men in one of our Batteries. The Sergeant was torn into several pieces, one of which landed on the top of the Officers' Mess and another in a gun pit 150 yards away. One of his legs could not be found, so they had to bury what they could, an incomplete set of torn fragments. But three or four days later the smell of the lost limb came drifting down a ravine above their guns, and following the scent, they found it, black with flies among the stones.

In my old Battery, too, four hundred cartridges went up with a direct hit, and the Austrians then shelled the smoke with unpleasant effect. A twelve-inch shell also burst very close to the Battery's

Mess, killing a number of Italian telephonists next door.

Throughout these days, periods of very heavy firing alternated with periods of comparative quiet.

.   .   .   .   .   .

On the 25th a party of nearly thirty British officers and men, a procession of two cars, three side-cars and twelve motor bicycles, went up Podgora Hill. The Italian Second Army, to whom we were strangers, watched us with interest as we went past in a cloud of dust. On the top of Podgora Hill was a series of O.P.'s, known collectively as Maria O.P., hollowed out of the rock, approached through rock passages, and in front a wide rocky platform commanding a splendid panorama. At our feet was a precipitous descent, clothed with acacias, at the bottom Podgora with its gutted factories, then the broad stream of the Isonzo, and Gorizia on the further side. To the left we could see the Isonzo winding down out of the mountains, between Monte Sabotino and Monte Santo, the latter hiding from our sight the Bainsizza Plateau. In the centre of our view rose the great mass of San Gabriele ; Italian patrols were out on its southern slopes, clearly visible through field-glasses. Then Santa Catarina and the long low brown hillside of San Marco. Away to the right the flat lands of the Isonzo and Vippacco valleys, and beyond these again the northern ridge of the Carso, from Dosso Faiti to the Stoll, beautifully visible. On the right everything seemed quiet, but there was tremendous Allied shelling of San Gabriele, Santa Catarina and San Marco. French Gunners also were here with fifteen-inch guns firing on San Marco, and two of their officers were at Maria O.P. that day. It was symbolic that from this height, for the first time on the Italian Front, Gunners of the three Western Allies were looking out eastward together toward the Promised Land.

The enemy trenches on San Marco lay out of view behind the crest, and our registration point, a white house on the top of the ridge, was almost completely blown away by a big French shell while we were watching, and waiting our turn to fire. We saw another shell burst in the Isonzo just above Gorizia, causing a huge waterspout. Colonel Canale arrived while we were firing. His white gloves were a little soiled, and he seemed rather worried and more serious than usual. He was disappointed at the stoppage of the offensive on the Carso.

·

CHAPTER XVI

THE FALL OF MONTE SANTO

EVEN when our guns were turned against San Marco, we continued to man Sant' Andrea O.P., for one could get good general observation to the northward from the other side of the ruined house which was the old O.P., and most of the trenches on San Marco were invisible except from aeroplanes. I spent the night there several times during the August offensive, watching by turns with one of our Bombardiers, to whom I explained that wars were made by small groups of wicked men, generally also rich, sitting

and planning in secret. I proposed to him the need
to shell such groups, while they were yet forming, with
the shrapnel of public opinion.

It was also at Sant' Andrea that I met a young
Lieutenant of Italian Field Artillery, a Sardinian
from Cagliari. He had still the face of a child, and
he had, too, that perfect self-possession and that
wonderful, soft charm which are so often found together in the Italian youth. I think of him often with
affection, and with an eager hope that he passed
unharmed through all the vicissitudes which were to
follow.

He and I spent many hours together, watching
those bloody, memorable hills. I met him first on
the 24th of August, and we drank a bottle of Vermouth together, and discussed with enthusiasm many
subjects. We even worked out in detail a scheme
for the interchange of students, for periods of a year
at a time, between Italian and British Universities
after the war. We then turned to modern history
and I noticed that he did not respond as much as I
had expected to the name of Garibaldi. He held the
historical theory that, broadly speaking, there are no
really great men, but only lucky ones. He put forward
in support of this view the distribution of death,
wounds and decorations in this war. This theory
of history has in it larger elements of wholesome-
ness and truth than has, for instance, the pernicious
bombast of Carlyle. I told my Sardinian friend that
I had once heard it said by a most learned man that,
if Rousseau had never lived, the world would not
look very different to-day, except that probably there
would be no negro republic in the island of Haiti.

This saying pleased him and he was inclined to think it plausible.

He told me that day that Monte Santo was reported taken, but the news was not yet sure.

.   .   .   .   .   .

I saw him again three days later and by then all the world knew that Monte Santo had fallen. For Cadorna in his communiqué of the 25th had cried: " Since yesterday our tricolour has been waving from the summit of Monte Santo ! " Already we could see the flashes of Italian Field Guns in action near the summit. All day I was buoyant, exhilarated, and as absorbed in the war as any journalist.

Victory has an intoxicating quality in this bright clear atmosphere, and among these mountains, which it has, perhaps, nowhere else. All day there seemed to be in the air a strange thrill, which at evening seemed to grow into a great throbbing Triumph Song of the Heroes,—incomparable Italians, living and dead. The emotion of it became almost unbearable.

" Our tricolour is waving from the summit of Monte Santo ! "

Here on the night of the 26th there occurred a scene wonderfully, almost incredibly, dramatic. The moon was rising. Shells passed whistling overhead, some coming from beyond the Isonzo toward the Ternova Plateau, others in the opposite direction from Ternova. Rifle shots rang out from beneath Monte Santo, along the slopes of San Gabriele, where the Italian and Austrian lines were very close together, where no word on either side might be spoken above a whisper. Suddenly there crashed out from the gloom the opening bars of the Marcia Reale, played

6

with tremendous *élan* by a military band.   The music
came from Monte Santo.   On the summit of the
conquered mountain, the night after its conquest,
an Italian band was playing amid the broken ruins
of the convent, standing around the firmly planted
Italian flag.   It was the Divisional Band of the four
Regiments which had stormed these heights.   On the
flanks of the mountain, along the new lines in the
valley beneath, along the trenches half-way up San
Gabriele, Italian soldiers raised a cry of startled joy.
Below the peak an Italian Regiment held the line
within forty yards of the enemy, crouching low in
the shallow trenches.   Their Colonel leaped to his
feet and his voice rang out, " Soldiers, to your feet !
Attention ! "   All along the trench the soldiers,
with a swift thrill of emotion, sprang to their feet.
Then again the Colonel cried, " My soldiers, let us cry
aloud in the face of the enemy, ' Long live Italy !
Long live the King ! Long live the Infantry ! ' "
Loud and long came the cheers, echoing and re-
echoing from the rocks, taken up and repeated by
others who heard them, first near at hand, then far
away, echoing and spreading through the night, like
the swelling waves of a great sea.

The Austrians opened fire on Monte Santo.   But
the music still went on.   The Marcia Reale was
finished, but now in turn the Hymn of Garibaldi and
the Hymn of Mameli, historic battle songs of Italian
liberty, pealed forth to the stars, loud above the
bursting of the shells.   And many Italian eyes, from
which the atrocious sufferings of this war had never
yet drawn tears, wept with a proud, triumphant joy.
And as the last notes died away upon the night air,

a great storm of cheers broke forth afresh from the Italian lines. The moon was now riding high in the heavens, and every mountain top, seen from below, was outlined with a sharp-cut edge against the sky.

Four days after, not far from this same spot, General Capello, the Commander of the Italian Second Army, decorated with the Silver Medal for Valour some of the heroes of the great victory. Among these was a civilian, a man over military age. It was Toscanini, Italy's most famous musical conductor. It was he who, charged with the organisation of concerts for the troops, had found himself in this sector of the Front when Monte Santo fell, and, hearing the news, had demanded and obtained permission to climb the conquered mountain. He reached the summit on the evening of the 26th and, by a strange chance, found his way among the rocks and the ruins of the convent, to the place where the band was playing. His presence had upon the musicians the same effect which the presence of a great General has upon faithful troops. They crowded round him, fired with a wild enthusiasm. Then Toscanini took command of what surely was one of the strangest concerts in the world, played in the moonlight, in an hour of glory, on a mountain top, which to the Italians had become an almost legendary name, to an audience of two contending Armies, amid the rattle of machine guns, the rumble of cannon, and the crashes of exploding shells.

.   .   .   .

" Our tricolour is waving from the summit of Monte Santo ! "

If the souls of poets be immortal and know what still passes in this world, be sure that the soul of Swinburne sings again to-day, from hell or heaven, the Song of the Standard.

" This is thy banner, thy gonfalon, fair in the front of thy
    fight,
  Red from the hearts that were pierced for thee, white as
    thy mountains are white,
  Green as the spring of thy soul everlasting, whose life-blood
    is light.
  Take to thy bosom thy banner, a fair bird fit for the nest,
  Feathered for flight into sunrise or sunset, for eastward or
    west,
  Fledged for the flight everlasting, but held yet warm to
    thy breast.
  Gather it close to thee, song-bird or storm-bearer, eagle
    or dove,
  Lift it to sunward, a beacon beneath to the beacon above,
  Green as our hope. in it, white as our faith in it, red as our
    love."

CHAPTER XVII

THE CONQUEST OF THE BAINSIZZA PLATEAU

THE Italian advance on the Middle Isonzo in the early days of the August offensive reached a depth of six miles on a front of eleven miles. The Italians had swept across the Bainsizza Plateau, and had gained observation and command, though not possession, of the Valley of Chiapovano, the main Austrian line of communication and supply in this sector. This advance and the resumption of the war of movement raised, for the moment, tremendous expectations, which were destined, alas, to die away without fulfilment.

The passage of the Isonzo, here a deep cleft in the mountains, from Plava to above Canale, had been accomplished by the combined skill and valour of Infantry, Artillery and Engineers. The preliminary work of the Engineers in roadmaking on the western side of the river had been, as always, worthy of the highest praise. A great mass of bridging material had had to be accumulated in the valley, alongside camouflaged roads. The Austrians must have been on their guard, but it seems probable that they did not expect a big attack to be made here. For they were fully conscious of the natural strength of their positions.

First to cross the river on the night of the attack were boats carrying Engineers and detachments of Arditi. As they crossed, the river gorge was full of mist and they were not detected. But when the work of bridging began, and sounds of hammering and the dragging of planks into position could be clearly heard, suddenly all along the further bank the Austrian machine guns began to spit fire, and red rockets went up calling for the Artillery barrage. Many boats were hit and sank, and the Bridging Detachments suffered severe casualties. One bridge, half built, was set on fire, and one could see·dark shadows, lit up by the glare amid the darkness, darting forward to extinguish the flames. Fourteen bridges were thrown across under heavy fire, and, as the Infantry began to cross, Platoon after Platoon, the Austrian Machine Gunners fired at the sound of their footsteps, and many Italians fell, especially officers leading their men. But the crossing went on and, when dawn broke, the attackers had a firm footing on the left bank of the river. They swept round the flanks of those machine guns which had not yet been put out of action, and making use of the subterranean passages which the enemy had pierced in the cliffs for sheltered communication between the higher and the lower levels of the mountain, began to pour forth upon the crest of the ridge which overlooks the river. Then, as the advance continued, the Austrian right wing above Canale gave way in confusion and the Italians pressed forward on to the Bainsizza Plateau.

But their difficulties were tremendous. When they left the valley of the Isonzo behind them, they entered a waterless land, without springs for some four miles. In the early stages of the battle all water for the troops had to be brought up by mules, and likewise all food, ammunition and medical supplies, until the Engineers could get to work with road-building on the left bank of the river. The Bainsizza Plateau itself, lying amid a mass of barren mountains, contains woods, pastures, springs, small villages, a few roads and many tracks. The Italians swept over it on the 21st and 22nd of August, but soon found themselves once more in difficult country. In the days that followed the advance was slower and more spasmodic, but it still continued. By the 27th, 25,000 Austrian prisoners had been taken, together with a great quantity of material, and several whole Austrian Divisions had ceased to exist.

It had been a wonderful feat of arms, finely conceived by the Staff, magnificently executed by the rank and file. It opened out a great vista of new possibilities, but, for the moment, it was over.   Before any further advance was practicable, the positions won had to be consolidated, roads had to be built, dumps and stores of every kind to be moved forward.

. . . . . .

In a village on the Bainsizza Plateau, half wrecked by shell fire, two old peasants were sitting outside their house.   Austrian shells whistled through the air and burst a few hundred yards away.   " These are not for us," said one of the old men to an Italian soldier, " the shells and the war are for the soldiers, not the civilians."

CHAPTER XVIII

THE FIGHTING DIES DOWN

ON the 28th of August the offensive was really beginning again.   We were firing on San Marco at a slow rate from six a.m. for an hour, then " vivace " from seven till noon, and at noon we lifted and continued vivace.   San Marco was not rocky, and the trenches there should be bombardable into pulp.   In the early morning from Sant' Andrea the hills all round were clearly outlined, except where some long belts of motionless, white, low-lying cloud partly hid the Faiti-Stoll range. Later, with the sun up, a warm haze hid everything. Firing continued heavy till six p.m., and then slowed down.   The attack on San Marco had failed.

Next day there was a good deal of shelling and some

torrential showers. We set fire to some woods on
the lower slopes of San Daniele, with a high wind
blowing.

.   .   .   .   .

The Battery's good luck continued. On the 30th,
while my Gun Detachment were at breakfast, a 5.9
burst in their shelter trench, at the moment un-
occupied, and covered every one with showers of loose
earth. All the breakfast vanished, and our shells
were thrown about like driftwood in a storm. But
no ammunition was exploded and no one was hurt.
Raven, who had been up Sabotino that day, told us
that " San Gabriele is tottering." Our offensive
seemed to have completely come to an end on the
Carso and in the Vippacco Valley. But we were still
hammering away at San Marco and San Gabriele,
at intervals of a few days at a time. On the 2nd of
September San Gabriele was still " tottering," on
the morning of the 4th it was reported taken, on the
6th we heard that it had been taken, lost and retaken,
the Arno Brigade having distinguished themselves
by some wonderful bombing. Cadorna's objective
now, it was said, was Lubiana, and not Trieste.
The Major and I both agreed that the Entente ought
to put every available man and tank on to this Front
and go for Vienna. On the 8th Raven told us that
the top of San Gabriele was held, but not the lower
slopes nor Santa Catarina, which were still precariously
supplied from behind San Marco. A few days later
we lost the top of San Gabriele, and the attack upon
it was not renewed.

Then followed quiet times, except for activity by
Austrian Trench Mortars against our trenches on

Hill 126. We established direct telephonic communication from the Battery to the Infantry Brigade Headquarters in order to provide rapid retaliation, and we made several Reconnaissances to try to locate Trench Mortars in the tangle of broken ground through which the enemy line ran.

On the 17th we were warned to be ready to move at short notice to the neighbourhood of Monfalcone, for a big push against the Hermada in three weeks' time. Battery positions were chosen, but we never went. Instead a rumour began to spread that all British Batteries were leaving Italy and going East. It was said that the War Office had the wind up about the Turks. An international tug of war was going on behind the scenes. On the afternoon of the 28th we were told on high authority that our movements were still undecided, but the Battery was inspected that day by General Capello, the victor of Bainsizza, who looked like an Eastern potentate, and was heard to say that he wanted as many British Batteries as he could get, to increase the gun power of the Second Army. That evening, however, our fate was said to be unofficially decided. We, with the rest of Raven's Group, five Batteries in all, were to stay in Italy, the other two Groups were to go away. It was not till the 3rd of October that we received definite orders on the subject. The other Groups went to Egypt and a couple of Batteries, after three months of doing nothing in Cairo, came back to Italy again. They had at any rate found a little employment for some of our surplus shipping and they had missed some queer experiences in Italy meantime.

It was also announced that we were not moving

down to Monfalcone, but were probably remaining
in our present positions for the winter.   We therefore
began systematically to prepare winter quarters.   The
Italian Corps Commander in a special Order of the
Day expressed his satisfaction that our Group was
remaining under his command.

.   .   .   .   .   .

On the 5th I got up at four o'clock in the morning
and carried out a Front Line Reconnaissance with
Sergeant Cotes, the No. 1 of my gun, and Avoglia,
an Italian Sergeant Major attached to our Battery,
rather a sleek person, who had been a *maître-d'hôtel*
at Brighton before the war.   We went along the
front line trenches on Hill 126, recently captured.
These trenches ran beside the river and were now
in fine condition, great repairs and reconstruction
having been carried out during the past three weeks.
It was here that Austrian Trench Mortars were active.
They were firing when we arrived and caused some
casualties.   As it grew light, a strong Austrian patrol
was seen moving about in No Man's Land, and it was
thought that a raid might be coming.   The order
" Stand to " was given, and the Infantry came swarming out of their dug-outs, a crowd of youths, some
very handsome, with almost Classical Roman features,
and older men, sturdy and bearded.   They densely
manned the parapet, with fixed bayonets and hand
grenades.   The machine gun posts were also manned.
But nothing happened !
A little later an Austrian was seen to emerge from
cover in No Man's Land, about a hundred yards
away from us, and run towards our trenches, throwing
away his rifle and shouting some unintelligible words.

He was sick of the war and wanted to surrender. But a young Italian recruit, in the trenches for the first time, quivering with excitement and eagerness to distinguish himself, not realising the man's motive, fired at him through a peephole. He missed, but the Austrian turned and doubled back like a rabbit to his own lines, where I suppose he was shot, poor brute, by his own people. I was standing quite close to the young recruit when he fired. No one rebuked him, but a Corporal patiently explained things to him. We smiled at one another, and I wished him " auguri " and went on up the hill.

The Austrian snipers were busy, and another Italian standing close to me, looking out slantwise through a peephole, was shot through the jaw. He was bandaged up, profusely bleeding, and went stoically down the hill, supported by a companion, leaving a red trail along the wooden duck-boards that paved the trench.

I went down two saps which the Italians had pushed out, one to within twenty yards, the other to within ten yards, of the Austrian front line. Here every one spoke in a low whisper or by signs. They warned me to keep well down, as the Austrians hated khaki worse even than " grigio-verde," as one is always apt to hate third parties who butt in against one in what one conceives to be a purely private quarrel.

But I went back armed with some useful information regarding the position of those Austrian Trench Mortars.

CHAPTER XIX

A LULL BETWEEN TWO STORMS

FROM the beginning of October the Battery were hard at work on their winter quarters. We had two large dining and recreation huts for the men, one for the Right Section and one for the Left, fitted up with long wooden tables and benches. These huts were dug into the bank, one on either side of the road leading up from the Battery position to Pec village. The dug-outs were improved and made watertight and the Officers' Mess and sleeping huts were moved up from the river bank into the Battery position itself. Everything was very comfortable and handy.

We maintained close relations with an Italian Battery next door commanded by a certain Captain Romano. His men helped us in putting up our huts, which were of Italian design, and we had frequent exchanges of hospitality. Romano was a Regular officer, about 28 years old, with twinkling brown eyes and a voice like a foghorn even when speaking from a short distance away, but a fine singer. He had a wonderful collection of photographs, was a good Gunner and popular with his men.

.   .   .   .   .   .

On the 9th I spent the night in Lecce O.P. on Hill 123, overlooking Hills 126 and 94. It was named after the Lecce Brigade who made it, one of the best Brigades in the Italian Army. When they were in front of us, we saw a good deal of them. Now the Parma Brigade were holding the line and the British officer in the O.P. used to take his meals at the Brigade Headquarters. Things were rather active that evening. At half-past five in the afternoon the enemy opened a heavy bombardment, increasing to a pitch of great fury, on our front and support trenches. Our own lines down below me were blotted out from sight by dense clouds of crashing, flashing smoke. Just before six the Italian Brigadier asked me for a heavy barrage from all the British Batteries. A big counter-bombardment was now working up from our side. I spoke on the telephone to Raven, who told me that all our Batteries were firing "*double vivace.*" At a quarter past six the Austrians attacked. There was a terrific rattle of Italian machine gun fire, almost drowning the sound of the heavier explosions, and a stream of rockets went up from our front line calling for more barrage. The attack was beaten off by machine guns and hand grenades. A few Austrians reached our parapet, but none got into our trenches.

Firing died down about a quarter to seven, and the Brigadier came up to the O.P., very pleased with the support we had rendered, and asked that a slow rate of fire might be kept up. Later on an Austrian telephone message was overheard, which suggested that the attack was to be renewed just before dawn, after a gas attack. We kept on the alert, but nothing happened. Two of our Batteries went on firing at a slow rate all night. When dawn broke, it was evident that our bombardment had been very destructive. The enemy's trenches were knocked to pieces ; uprooted trees, planks, sandbags and dead bodies lay about in confusion. It was thought that owing to our fire some Austrian units, which were to have taken part in the attack, could not, and others would not, do so, in spite of a special issue of rum and other spirits. I saw also, motionless amid the Austrian wire, a figure in Italian uniform, one of a patrol who had gone out four nights before, and had not returned.

.   .   .   .   .   .

On the 12th I went out with a Sergeant, a Signaller and Corporal Savogna, a Canadian Italian, on a Front Line Reconnaissance on the northern side of the Vippacco, in the Second Army area. The day was wonderfully clear and we could see the everlasting snows beyond Cadore. We went through Rupa to Merna and, being evidently spotted, were shelled with 4.2's and forced to proceed along a muddy communication trench knee deep in water. At Raccogliano Mill we visited the Headquarters of the Bergamo Brigade, which was holding the line. A guide took us along the front line, which had been considerably advanced here in August and September, and again by a successful local attack a few days before. We went down one *Caverna* in which, on the occasion of this last attack, a Magyar officer and 25 men surrendered. The Austrian sentry, also a Magyar, had been fastened by the leg to the doorpost outside the entrance to the dug-out. In the Italian bombardment one of his feet was blown away, but his own people had done nothing for him. Now his dead body lay out in the open behind the new Italian front line.

.   .   .   .

On the 14th Jeune went on leave to England, no one having any expectation that anything of importance was likely to happen in the near future. In his absence I acted as Second-in-Command of the Battery.

On the 19th we heard that the Italian High Command was preparing another big offensive from the Bainsizza against the Ternova Plateau, and the same day the Intelligence Report contained the information that a series of German Divisions had been seen detraining at Lubiana since the beginning of October, and that, owing to the Russian collapse, a thousand Austrian guns had been moved across from the Russian to the Isonzo Front since the middle of September. We had noticed a perceptible increase in the enemy's Artillery activity for some time, but this, we thought at the time, was purely defensive. There had also been a week of heavy rains, but the Vippacco, after rising rapidly and threatening to flood us all out, fell eighteen inches in one night. It swept away a number of Italian bridges, however, from Merna and Raccogliano further up stream, and we saw pieces of these rushing past in the swift current.

On the 21st the Major and I motored to Palmanova and bought some winter clothing at the Ordnance. An Austrian twelve-inch howitzer, whom we had christened " Mr Pongo," was shelling all day at intervals, chiefly in the back areas. An unpleasant beast, we agreed, who wanted smothering !

On the 22nd it was evident, from the Austrian shelling, that quite a number of fresh heavy howitzers, both twelve- and fifteen-inch, had appeared behind the Austrian lines. A few, no doubt, of those thousand guns from Russia ! Listening to their shells whistling over one's head like express trains, and to their (happily distant) deep crashes on percussion, one realised very vividly the immediate military effects of the Russian collapse. We heard that the Italian offensive was not coming off after all.

On the 23rd we heard that a big Austrian attack was expected last night and might come that night instead. We received orders to clean up and prepare, in case of necessity, the old position at Boschini on San Michele, which the Battery had occupied when they first arrived in Italy. This, I thought, seemed rather panic-stricken. Romano's Battery had similar orders. It would be annoying to leave our present position after all the work put into it to make it habitable for the winter. But I noted that the atmosphere was tinged with apprehension.

PART IV

THE ITALIAN RETREAT AND RECOVERY

CHAPTER XX

THE BEGINNING OF THE ENEMY OFFENSIVE

ON the morning of October 24th soon after nine o'clock the enemy launched a big attack against the Third Army Front, especially violent between Faiti and the Vippacco, and renewed it in the afternoon. But he gained no ground. All through the previous night and all that day till evening the bombardment on both sides was heavy. We had not fired during the night but began at seven in the morning and went on throughout the day. A message came in that the enemy would probably shell Batteries for four hours with gas shell, starting with irritant gas and going on to poison. He had already employed these tactics up north, as we learned later. Gas alert was on all night and we were listening strainedly for soft bursts. Heavy rain came down steadily all day, and everything was drenched and dripping. The spaces between our huts filled with water, and needed continual baling out. But when gas was expected, one welcomed heavy rain [1] and high winds and loud explosions from bursting shells.

[1] It was not till a later date that gases were employed, the effects of which were increased by rain.

Between nine and ten p.m. I heard a series of soft bursts just across the river and arranged with Romano's Battery for mutual alarms if any gas should come too near. An hour later I was relieved in the Command Post and turned in. As I was undressing, I heard the wind rising again and the telephonists next door baling out their dug-out. We were keeping up a desultory fire all night to harass any further attacks that might be attempted. The Major, who had been out on a Front Line Reconnaissance that morning in the neighbourhood of Merna, had come in for some very heavy shelling and returned very weary.

.   .   .   .   .   .

The next day, the 25th, was at least fine; it was even rather sunny. We did a little firing, but not much, between seven a.m. and two p.m. Enemy planes came over continually, flying very low, about thirty in the course of the morning. They attacked one of our observation balloons, which descended rapidly as they approached, and I think got down safely. Italian anti-aircraft guns brought down one of them. Whenever we shelled Mandria, a little village up the valley, a plane came over. Evidently they had something there as to which they were sensitive, perhaps a General's Billet!

At half past ten the Italians ditched a lorry full of ammunition just at the top of the road from the Battery position to Pec village, in full view of the enemy on Hill 464. At this time the village was being heavily shelled by 5.9's, and our cookhouse on the outskirts was all but hit, shells bursting all round it in a circle. Showers of bricks and lumps of earth

and masonry rose high in the air. One shell hit
the Artillery Group Headquarters of Major Borghese
and I saw all his office papers going up, a cloud of
shreds, shining in the sun. I laughed and said to
myself, " There goes a lot of red tape ! " I saw
Borghese himself later in the day limping along with a
stick ; a chunk of one of his office walls had fallen on
his foot.

The enemy meanwhile had begun to shell the lorry,
methodically as their idiotic habit was, with one shell
every five minutes. It was too near us to be pleasant,
so the Major took out a party and hauled it out of
their view under cover of a bank. But this took some
time. Leary stood by with a stopwatch calling out
the minutes. At the end of every fourth minute, the
party ran for cover. Then a few seconds later we
heard the next shell coming. The Major was hit on
the hand once by a shell splinter which drew blood,
but nothing more serious than this happened.

About two o'clock a big bombardment worked up
again, and the Volconiac and Faiti became a sea of
smoke and flame. This went on till dusk, we firing
hard all the time. More enemy planes came over,
one even after dark, a most unusual thing, flying very
low indeed, under a heavy fire of anti-aircraft Batteries
and machine guns from the ground. Our planes had
been very scarce all day. They had nearly all gone
north. For the time being we had quite lost the
command of the air in this sector.

The two British Batteries who were furthest forward
had orders to move back that night to reserve positions
on San Michele. The Italians were going to horse
their guns, for it was said that the majority of the

tractors had gone north too. This move looked
rather panicky, I thought.

Many red rockets went up in the early evening from
Volconiac and Faiti. The enemy were making another
attack. Then a little later tricolour rockets, red, white
and green, went up. This was the signal that the
attack had been beaten off and that the situation was
quiet again. The firing died down about seven. We
fed and put up for the night an Italian officer, whose
Battery used to be here, but had moved north yesterday. He had just come back from a gas course at
Palmanova. From a newspaper which he had I saw
that a strong offensive had begun on the afternoon of
the 23rd to the north of the Bainsizza Plateau. Either
the attacks here were only holding attacks, or the
attack to the north was a feint and the real thing was
to be here. Anyhow, I thought, it is their Last
Despairing Great Cry! I turned in just after midnight. The night was still and there was a bright
moon and stars. A thick mist lay along the Vippacco,
just behind the trees. The air was damp and cold.
It seemed pretty quiet for the moment all along the
Front.

.   .   .   .   .   .

I had a troubled night. In the early morning we
were bombarded with gas shell and had to wear
respirators from a quarter to three till four o'clock.
We were firing from five till six and again steadily
from a quarter past seven onwards. We got orders
to move back that night to Boschini, on San Michele.
I thought this a great mistake. Later in the day our
move was cancelled, as the two forward Batteries
which pulled out last night would not be in action

on San Michele till to-morrow. They had been last heard of stuck fast in a crush of traffic at the bottom of the hill at Peteano. A strong team of horses were straining their guts out in vain attempts to pull an Italian twelve-inch mortar up the hill. It was this which had caused the block. Those two forward Batteries *might* have lost their guns in a quick retreat, I thought, but hardly we. It seemed to be feared, however, that the two bridges across the Vippacco might go.

That day we were shelled heavily with every kind of weapon, from fifteen-inch downwards, especially the Left Section in the afternoon. We had, as usual, marvellously good luck, and only had one casualty, and that a slight wound. The spirit and endurance of the men were wonderful. Enemy planes were over all day ; we counted twenty-two between daybreak and four p.m. Some hovered overhead and ranged their guns on us. Several times we put our detachments under cover and ceased fire owing to the shelling. My own gun was half buried by a great shower of earth kicked up by a 9.45, which pitched right on top of the bank in front of us. But Cotes, my Sergeant, and myself, crouching under cover of the girdles, were quite unhurt. The rest of the detachment had been ordered down into their dug-out. Another time the enemy neatly bracketed our Command Post with twelve-inch, and several of us within were uncomfortably awaiting the next round. But luckily for us he switched away to the right.

We had to fire hard most of the day, especially in the afternoon and evening. It had been exhausting and almost sleepless work for the detachments for

several days past, for Darrell and a working party of
forty were away preparing the reserve position on San
Michele, and we had hardly any reliefs for the guns.
The Major, too, looked very tired and frayed, but,
whenever our eyes met, he gave me a smile of encouragement and leadership. That evening, during
a short break in the firing, he asked me, since he
himself could not leave the Command Post, to go
round and " buck the men up " and thank them on
his behalf for the way in which they had behaved.
" So long as the Major's pleased, we're satisfied," said
one man. Another, a Bombardier who afterwards
got a Commission, and had been with Darrell on a
reconnaissance on Faiti a few days before and had
nearly been killed on the journey, said, " Well, Sir,
we were thinking of the boys in the Front Line to-
day." And well he might, for it had been a hellish
bombardment up there. After delivering my message
to the men, I walked up and down the road in front
of the guns for a few moments in the short silence,
realising how the Alliance of Britain and Italy was
burning itself more deeply than ever into our hearts
in these days of trial.

.   .   .   .   .   .

That night the enemy attacked again, and we lost
Faiti and Hill 393, and had to fire on them. I heard
afterwards from the Group that Colonel Canale, when
he gave the order to fire on 393, was almost weeping
on the telephone. Next day we counter-attacked
and retook Faiti, but 393 remained in Austrian hands.
Rumours and denials of rumours came in from the
north. It was said that we had lost Monte Nero and
Caporetto, and that German Batteries had kept up

a high concentration of gas for four hours on our lines in the Cadore. And we knew that the Italian gas masks were only guaranteed to last for an hour and a half in such conditions, and that each man only carried one.

CHAPTER XXI

FROM THE VIPPACCO TO SAN GIORGIO DI NOGARA

ON the 27th the rumours became bad. The German advance to the north was said to be considerable and rapid. Orders came that all the British Batteries were to pull out and park that night at Villa Viola, behind Gradisca, " for duty on another part of the Front." Probably, we thought, we were going north. " The gun concentration up there must be awful," said the Major. I told Cotes that we were probably going into the thick of it, and his eyes shone with pride. He was a fine fellow. That day the sun was shining, and the Italian planes in this sector seemed to have regained command of the air. For the moment there was a little lull in the firing, but we felt that some big fate was looming over us. I went away to my hut for five minutes and wrote in my diary, " I here put it on record once more that I am proud to fight in and for Italy. I repeat that dying here is not death, it is flying into the dawn ! If I die in and for Italy, I would like to think that my death would do something for Anglo-Italian sympathy and understanding."

In the early afternoon the Major went down to

Headquarters. He rang me up from there to say that two guns were to be pulled out at once, and the other two to double their rate of fire. No. 4 gun was now engaging two different targets with alternate rounds and different charges.

When the Major came back, he called all the men together and said. " I am not going to conceal anything from you. The situation is serious. The Italians have had a bad reverse up north. But there is no need for anyone to get panicky. We shall pull out and go back to-night. That is all I know at present. When I know more, I will tell you more. One gun will remain in action till the last. No. 2 is the easiest to get out, so I have chosen her for the post of honour." As the men scattered, I heard several saying, " Good old No. 2 ! "

The Major told me that the Austrians were almost in Cividale, staggering news. Tractors and lorries were to come and take away our guns and stores in the evening. But the number of tractors was very limited and Raven was doubtful if enough would come in time. The whole Third Army was retreating, and three British Batteries, ourselves, the Battery in Pec village and the Battery at Rupa, would be the last three Batteries of Medium or Heavy Calibre left on this part of the Front.

All through the afternoon and evening Italian Infantry and Artillery were retreating through Pec. Some looked stolid, others depressed, others merely puzzled. But a little later a Battalion came along the road the other way, going up to be sacrificed on Nad Logem. They halted to rest by the roadside, full of gaiety and courage. They cheered our men on No. 2

gun, who were pumping out shells as fast as they could.
" Bravi inglesi ! " cried the Italians, and some of our
men replied, " Good luck, Johnny ! " Unknown
Italians were always " Johnny."

As the dark came on, ammunition dumps began
to go up everywhere ; the Italians were deliberately
exploding them, and great flashes of light, brighter
than even an Italian noonday, lit up the whole sky
for minutes at a time. Romano's Battery next door
to us threw the remains of their ammunition into the
river, and pulled out and away about 6.30. They
were horse-drawn and did not need to wait for tractors.
We wished each other good-bye, and hoped we might
meet again some better day. We too got orders to
destroy all ammunition we could not fire, as there
would be no transport to take it away. So we gave
No. 2 a generous ration and heaved the rest into the
waters of the Vippacco.

No. 2 went on firing ceaselessly. So did one gun
of the Battery in the village, and one gun at Rupa.
That Battery, being the furthest forward, was in the
greatest danger of the three. About 7 o'clock our
first tractor arrived and took away No. 1 gun with
Winterton and Manzoni. Enemy bombing planes
came over frequently. One came right over us and
then turned down the Vallone, and there was a series
of heavy explosions, and great clouds of brownish
smoke leapt up beneath her track.

Why, I kept asking myself, didn't the fools shell
Pec village, where a crowd of men and guns were
waiting for transport ? Why didn't they put over
gas shell ? Why didn't they bomb us ? Evidently
there were no Germans *here* ! About a quarter to nine

No. 2 finished her ammunition, and we pulled her out.
The other three guns had gone now and the other two
British Batteries were clear, all but two lorries. Just
after nine o'clock our last tractor came along and
took off No. 2, with Darrell in charge of her. How
the Italians had managed to get all these lorries and
tractors for us, I don't know, for, in the Third Army
as a whole, they were terribly short of transport.
Many made the criticism that we should have kept
out in Italy our own transport. But the Italians
certainly did us very handsomely, at the cost of losing
some bigger guns of their own.

After the last British gun had ceased to fire there
was for about five minutes an eerie stillness, as though
all our Artillery had gone and theirs was holding its
fire. And then an Italian Field Battery opened again
on the right of Pec. For over an hour now I had
been expecting, minute by minute, to see the enemy
Infantry come swarming along the Nad Logem in the
dusk, cutting off our retreat, for I knew we had nothing
but rear-guards left up there. But they did not come!

Only the Major and I and about forty men were left
now, and we had been told that there would be no more
transport. So we destroyed everything that we had
been unable to get away, and the Major informed
Headquarters of the situation and then disconnected
the telephone and the men fell in and we marched away.
We were just in time to see an Italian Field Battery
come into Pec at the gallop, the gunners all cheering,
unlimber their guns, take up position and open fire.
It was a smart piece of work, done with a real Latin
gesture. How enfuriating it was to be leaving these
wooden huts of ours and these good positions, on

which had been spent so many hours of labour, where we could have passed such a comfortable winter, going forth now none knew whither! Old Natale, one of the Italians attached to us, chalked up in German on the entrance to one of the huts, " You German pigs, we shall soon be back again ! " But at that moment I did not feel so sure. Natale was afterwards lost in the retreat, and was reported by us as " missing." But one of our men saw him again six months later with an Italian Battery and said he looked several years younger !

We passed Campbell, the Medical Officer, standing outside his dug-out on the road. He was waiting for the last of the other Batteries' parties to get away. He told me afterwards that we were out only just in time. Within half an hour of our going, the Austrians fairly plastered the position with shells of all calibres. They shelled the road a little as we went along, but not too much. As we passed the railway embankment at Rubbia, we saw and spoke to some Italian machine-gunners in position, whose orders were to hold up the enemy till the last possible moment. They were quite calm and determined, those boys, knowing perfectly well that, by the time the enemy came, the Isonzo bridges would have been blown up behind them. I dragged myself on with an aching heart. One who retreats cuts a poor figure beside a rear-guard that stays behind and fights.

We crossed the Isonzo at Peteano, and took a short cut across the fields to Farra. In the crowd and the dark we were jostled by some Italian Infantry. We hailed them and found that they were our old friends, the Lecce Brigade. The Major made our men stand

back. " Pass, Lecce," he said. " Good luck to you ! "
We marched on through Farra to Gradisca, both
blazing in the night. The towns and villages everywhere in this sector had been deliberately fired by the
retreating Italians, in addition to the ammunition
dumps. The whole countryside was blazing and
exploding. I thought of Russia in 1812, and the
Russian retreat before Napoleon, and Tchaikovsky's
music

It began to rain, but that made no difference to the
burning. In Gradisca burning petrol was running
about the streets. Earlier in the evening there had
been a queer scene here. The Headquarters of the
British Staff had been at Gradisca, and the Camp
Commandant had made a hobby of fattening rabbits
for the General's Mess. When the time had come
that day to pack up and go, it was found that the
lorries provided were fully loaded with office stores,
Staff officers' bulky kit and 20,000 cigarettes, which
the General was specially proud of having saved from
his canteen. There was no room for the Camp
Commandant's rabbit hutches, so these were opened
and the fat inmates released, to the delight of the
civilians and Italian soldiery in Gradisca, who knocked
them over or shot them as they ran. I heard this
from a gunner, who was officer's servant to one of the
Staff and witnessed the scene.

A few miles away, at the Ordnance Depôt at Villa
Freifeldt, thousands of pounds' worth of gun stores
stood ready, packed in crates, to be removed. But
no transport came for them, and they were abandoned
and fell into Austrian hands. For lack of them, our
Batteries were afterwards kept out of action for several

weeks. Whoever ordered these things seems to have thought it more important to save the Staff's kit and the General's cigarettes.

Just before we entered Gradisca, we passed a Battalion of the Granatieri, the Italian Grenadiers, all six foot tall, with collar badges of crimson and white, coming up from reserve to fight a rear-guard action. I had seen them a few days before in rest billets and admired their appearance. And in their march that night and in their faces was scorn for fugitives and contempt for death. The Major said to me, as they swung past us, that *that* Battalion could be trusted to fight to the end. And they did. Some of our men met a few of their survivors at Mestre a week later. Nearly the whole Battalion had been killed or wounded, but they had held up the Austrian advance for several hours.

On the further side of Gradisca we passed a great platform, which had been erected a few weeks before for the Duke of Aosta's presentation of medals for the Carso offensive. It was here that the Major had received the Italian Silver Medal for Valour. The platform looked ironical that night, still decked with bunting, limp and drenched now by the rain, and lit up by the flames of the burning town. We reached Villa Viola about 11.30 p.m. It was to have been a rendezvous, but there was no one there. Only the rain still falling. About midnight we entered an empty house, and threw ourselves down upon the floor to sleep.

. . . . . .

We had slept for less than an hour, when we were hurriedly awakened. The Italians had orders to set fire to the house. Meanwhile Savogna, our Canadian Italian Corporal, had just returned from scouting for us, and reported that parties from the other Batteries were in a house half a mile away. We marched off again through pouring rain, our path lit up by the flames, which in places thrust their long tongues right across the road. The wind blew clouds of smoke in our faces. The air was full of the roaring of the fires, the crackle of blazing woodwork, the crash of houses falling in, the loud explosions of ammunition dumps and petrol stores, which now and again for a few seconds lighted up the whole night sky for miles around with a terrific glare, and then died down again. Far as the eye could reach the night was studded with red and golden fires. Everywhere behind the front of the retreating Third Army a systematic destruction was being carried out. The Third Army was retreating in good order, unbroken and undefeated, retreating only because its northern flank was in danger of being turned. The Third Army was proving to the enemy that its movements were deliberate and governed by a cool purpose. The enemy should advance into a wilderness.

Again I seemed to hear in the air the music of " 1812," and the bells of burning Moscow ringing out loud and clear above the triumph song of the invader.

.   .   .   .   .   .

Our men marched doggedly on, some looking puzzled and full of wonder, others tired but cheerful, others with expressionless, · uncomprehending faces. But in the faces of a few I read a consciousness of the tremendous tragedy of which we formed a tiny part.

We found the other Batteries in a house not yet marked down for burning. The house was crowded out already and all the best places taken, such as they were. There were pools of water everywhere on the floor. Officers of the Group were there, knowing nothing, awaiting the appearance of Colonel Raven. All our party got in somehow and lay down to sleep. But half an hour later we were roused again. Raven had come and ordered that all should push on to Palmanova.

Some of our men were sleeping very heavily and were hard to waken. When we started it was still raining. The roads were crowded with traffic, including many guns. Our own went by with the rest, Winterton, Darrell, Leary and Manzoni with them. Each Battery party marched independently, the easier to get through blocks in the traffic. The Square at Palmanova had been fixed as the next rendezvous.

The stream of refugees with their slow-moving wagons drawn by oxen, or their little donkey carts, or trudging on foot carrying bundles, became gradually thicker and more painful. For we were back now in country that yesterday or the day before had fancied itself remote from the battle zone. I remember one elderly peasant woman, tall and erect as a young girl, with white hair and a face like Dante, calm, beautiful and stern. She was alone, tramping along through the mud. And she had the walk of a queen.

At Versa we halted for a few minutes at the Hospital. All the wounded had been evacuated.[1] Campbell

---

[1] One wounded British soldier, who had been in an Italian Field Hospital which was not evacuated in time, was taken prisoner by the Austrians. He told me, when he was released a year later,

was lying on a bed in one of the empty wards, snatching a little rest. He had seen the last British troops away from Pec and had then followed on a motor-bicycle. I went into the old R.A.M.C. Mess to see if any food or drink was left. The question of food was beginning to be serious for the whole retreating Army. Italian troops were clearing out everything. I found a wine bottle half full, and took a deep drink. It was vinegar, but it bucked one up. I handed the bottle to an Italian, and told him it was " good English wine." He drank a little, saw the joke, smiled and passed it on to an unsuspecting companion. I got a little milk which I shared with the Major and some of our men. Then we resumed the march.

We reached Palmanova about 7 a.m. It was now the 28th of October. We met Raven in the Square, where were also collected a British General and his Staff officers. They were standing about, with a half lost look on their faces. There was no evidence of decision or any plan. The General was smiling, as his habit was. The Staff Captain was telling someone, in a hopeless voice, that he had heard that the Italians were going back to the Tagliamento. Just as we arrived, the Italians began to set fire to the town. Dense clouds of black smoke, fanned by a strong wind, began to pour over our heads. Flames were soon roaring round houses, where three months ago I had been a guest. But the inmates had all gone now. Food and drink was being sold in the shops at knock-down prices. The Italian military authorities were

---

that the Austrians bayoneted the Italian wounded whom they found in this hospital, but spared the British, and, on the whole, treated them well.

requisitioning all bread, and issued some to us. The Major ordered it to be kept in reserve.

I went round the town and into the Railway Station looking for our guns. But there was no sign of them. I came back and slept for an hour amid some rubble under the archway inside one of the town gates. The town was burning furiously. Our men, wet to the skin, sheltered themselves from the smoke and the cold wind in the dry moat outside the walls.

Then the order came to move on. We formed up and started with the rest. Nobody knew whither. Some said Latisana, but no one knew how far off this was. The men had no rations except the bread obtained at Palmanova, and no prospect, apparently, of getting any. The Supply Officers of the A.S.C. might as well have gone to Heaven, for all the use they were to us during those days of retreat. It was raining again and the roads were blocked. We proceeded slowly for a mile or two, and were then turned off the road into a damp, open field, which someone said was a " strategic point." Here a number of different Battery parties collected. We were to wait for the guns. The downpour steadily increased, the field rapidly became a marsh, and there was no shelter anywhere. Raven walked up and down, puffing at this pipe, taking the situation with admirable calm. It was at this time that I personally touched my bedrock of misery, both mental and physical. For there seemed to be nothing to be done, and, what most irked me, there were so many senior officers present that I myself could take no decisions. Then some of our guns arrived, and were halted at the side of the road to wait for the rest. But this made the traffic

8

block worse, and they had to move forward again, and
the idea of getting them all together was abandoned.

Raven then gave the order to the rest of us to move
on.   There were some vacant places in various cars
and lorries at this point and some footsore men were
put in.   The Major insisted, in spite of my protests
that I preferred to walk, that I should get into one
of the cars, which I shared with Littleton, the Chaplain
who had thought that war " might be tremendously
worth while " and three junior officers from Raven's
Headquarters.   I was, in truth, pretty done at this
stage, chiefly through want of sleep, compared to
which I always found want of food a trifling incon-
venience.   It was now about 4 p.m. and we could
only make very slow progress.   A rendezvous had
been fixed by Raven at Foglie, where rations were to
have been distributed.   But there was no one and
no rations there, and it seemed that Raven had taken
the wrong road.   The enemy were said to be advancing from the north at right angles to our only possible
line of retreat, and the chances seemed strongly in
favour of our all being cut off.

An Italian doctor ran out into the road and stopped
our car, almost beside himself with despair.   He had
been left in charge of a number of severely wounded
cases, without any food, medical necessities or transport.   But we had no food and could do nothing to
help him, except promise to try to have transport
sent back to him from San Giorgio di Nogara.

CHAPTER XXII

FROM SAN GIORGIO TO THE TAGLIAMENTO

WE reached San Giorgio about 9 p.m. and here I got out of the car, which two of Raven's Staff took on to try and arrange for transport to be sent back for the Italian wounded. Having slept for an hour or two in the car, I felt quite a different being and fit for anything. Stragglers were coming in from the various Batteries' dismounted parties, and I collected nearly a hundred of these men into a hall on the ground floor of an Italian Field Hospital. They lay about on the stone floor, sleeping like logs. Upstairs a panic had spread among the wounded that they would be abandoned. Men were crying with terror and struggling to get out of bed. Campbell, who had now joined us, went up and helped the Italian medical personnel. Soon afterwards ambulances of both the Italian and British Red Cross began to arrive, and the hospital was quickly cleared. From one British Red Cross Driver I got a large box of Cabin biscuits, which I distributed among our men, some of whom were ravenously hungry. I also found a tap of good drinking water in the main street and here we refilled all available water bottles, including those of several men who were too fast asleep to waken.

The question then arose what to do with these stragglers. I went to the station, but found that no more trains were running. Latisana was said

to be only " a few kilometres " away. It was in fact
more than twenty. I discovered that it was on the
Tagliamento and I supposed that, once across the
river, we should be momentarily safe from risk of
capture, and, if ammunition was forthcoming, our
Batteries might once more come into action. Meanwhile we should push on as soon as possible. On the
other hand the men were very tired, having been
marching for twenty-four hours, with only a few
short breaks. A few hours' sleep now might be
worth a lot to them later on.

Several civilians came up to me and asked when
the Germans would be here. " This is my house,"
one old man explained, pointing to a small house near
the Hospital, " and I shall have to leave everything
if I go away. But I cannot stay . . . ," and he
began to cry.

In the early hours of the 29th I put some of our
most footsore stragglers on to lorries going in the
direction of Latisana. The rest marched off under
Henderson, one of the officers from Raven's Headquarters, who had come with me in the car to San
Giorgio. Meanwhile I was keeping a look-out for our
guns in the dense columns of traffic slowly crawling
past. I saw guns belonging to other Batteries, and
was told that some of ours were further behind. It
was just getting light, when a tractor appeared
drawing two of our guns and one belonging to another
British Battery, which we had picked up on the road
a long way back with only three gunners in charge of
it, and which would certainly have been lost, if we
had not taken it in tow. But, as the result of this
additional load, our tractor had been breaking down

all the way along, and had fallen almost to the rear of the retreating column. It had a damnable and useless accumulator, but there was no means of changing this. With the tractor and guns were Winterton, Darrell, and Leary, also the Battery Quartermaster Sergeant and two of our lorries. They told me Manzoni was well on ahead with the other two guns and I told them that the Major and the bulk of the dismounted party must also be a good distance ahead, as stragglers from this party had appeared here many hours before.

We were now the last British guns on the road, a post of honour which we continued to hold. I was delighted to find that I was now entitled, by reason of seniority, to take command. I sent on the two lorries with Winterton and Darrell, to get in touch as soon as possible with the two guns in front and the Major's party. Leary and I remained behind with the tractor and its load. We had about thirty men with us and a small quantity of rations, including a little tea. We moved on slowly and got stuck in a bad block of traffic at San Giorgio cross roads. Here we had to remain stationary for several hours. The dawn was breaking and we made some tea.

About 5 a.m. I got tired of sitting still and walked about half a mile down the road to find out the cause of the block. I began to control and jerrymander the traffic and at first annoyed an Italian officer, who was there with the same object as myself; but I persuasively pointed out to him the benefits to both of us, if we could only succeed in getting a move on, and he then calmed down and began to help me. In the end we both manœuvred our own transport into a moving stream, and went forward smiling.

We went along at a fine pace for several miles and then our tractor stopped and wouldn't start up again. Whereupon there came to our assistance a young man named Rinaldo Rinaldi, a skilled and resourceful mechanic, who was driving a tractor in rear of us. He patched up our engine and got us going again. But we kept on breaking down after intervals never very long. Time after time Rinaldo Rinaldi came running up, smiling and eager to help. He patched us up and got us going six times. But at last he had to pass us and go on. For he, too, was drawing guns. I shall never forget Rinaldo Rinaldi and the cheerful help he gave us. In the end he left us an accumulator, but it was not much better than our own.

Enemy planes now began to appear in the sky, some scouting only, others dropping bombs. They did more damage to the wretched refugees than to the military. What chances they missed that day! Once or twice, when we were stationary, I gave the order to scatter in the fields to left and right of the road. But they never came very near to hitting us. They flew very high and their markmanship was atrocious.

Atrocious also was our tractor! Finally, when it broke down and we had no fresh accumulator, we had to unlimber the front gun, attach drag ropes to the tractor, haul vigorously on the ropes until the engine started up, then back the tractor and front limber back to the guns, limber up, cast off the ropes and go ahead again. We did this three or four times in the course of an hour, and enjoyed the sense of triumphing over obstacles. But it was very laborious, and the intervals between successive breakdowns grew ominously shorter and shorter. And the last time the trick didn't work, though we had all heaved and heaved till we were very near exhaustion. We were fairly stuck now, half blocking the road. Great excitement, as was only natural, developed among those behind us.

I sent forward an orderly with a message to the Major, describing our plight and asking that, if possible, another tractor might be sent back from Latisana to pull us. This message never reached the Major, but was opened by another Field officer, who sent back this flatulent reply. " If you are with Major Blinks, you had better ask him whether you may use your own discretion and, if necessary, remove breech blocks and abandon guns." I was not with Major Blinks, and I neither knew nor cared where he might be. Nor had I any intention of abandoning the guns. I determined, without asking anyone's permission, to use my discretion in a different way.

I saw, a little distance in front, an Italian Field Artillery Colonel in a state of wild excitement. He was rushing about with an unopened bottle of red wine in his hand, waving it ferociously at the heads of refugees, and driving them and their carts off the road down a side track. A queer pathetic freight some of these carts carried, marble clocks and blankets, big wine flasks and canaries in cages. The Colonel had driven off the road also a certain Captain Medola, of whom I shall have more to say in a moment, and who was sitting sulkily on his horse among the civilian carts. The Colonel's object, it appeared, was to get

a number of Field Batteries through.   He had cleared
a gap in the blocked traffic and his Field Guns were
now streaming past at a sharp trot.   But he was an
extraordinary spectacle and made me want to laugh.
Treading very delicately, I approached this enfuriated
man, and explained the helpless situation of our guns,
pointing out that we were also unwillingly impeding
the movements of his own.   I asked if he could order
any transport to be provided for us.   He waved his
bottle at me, showed no sign of either civility or
comprehension, only screaming at the top of his voice,
" Va via, va via ! " [1]

I gave him up as hopeless, and went back to my
guns, intending to wait till he had disappeared and
things had quieted down again, and then to look for
help elsewhere.   But the Latin mind often follows
a thread of order through what an Anglo-Saxon is apt
to mistake for a mere hurricane of confused commotion.
Within five minutes Captain Medola came up to me
and said that the Colonel had ordered him to drag
our tractor and guns.   Medola was in command of
a Battery of long guns, and had one of these attached
to a powerful tractor on the road in front of us.   To
this long gun, therefore, we now attached our tractor,
useless as a tractor but containing valuable gun stores,
and our three guns.   It was a tremendous strain for
one tractor, however strong, to pull, and we decided
a little later to abandon our own tractor and most
of its contents.

Medola, having handed over his horse to an orderly,
who was to ride on ahead and arrange for a fresh
supply of petrol for his tractors, of which there were

[1] " Away with you, away with you ! "

three, mounted the front of the leading tractor and I got up beside him. He rendered us most invaluable help in a most willing spirit and at considerable risk to himself. For he undoubtedly had to go much more slowly with us in tow than he could have gone if he had been alone.

We saw another Battery of Italian heavy guns going along the road, heavier than either ours or Medola's. They were an ancient type, which we had seen sometimes on the Carso, and not of very high military value. But their gunners took a regimental and affectionate pride in those old guns. They had neither tractors nor horses, but they had dragged their beloved pieces for thirty miles from the rocky heights of the Carso, along good roads and bad, up and down hill, through impossible traffic blocks, down on to the plains as far as Palmanova, with nothing but long ropes and their own strong arms. They had forty men hauling on each gun. At Palmanova new hauling parties had been put on, who dragged the guns another thirty miles to the far side of the Tagliamento at Latisana. And as they hauled, they sang, until they were too tired to go on singing, and could only raise, from time to time, their rhythmical periodic cry of " Sforza ! . . . Sforza ! " [1]

.   .   .   .   .   .

As we passed through Muzzano, the town and road were heavily bombed. The bell in the campanile jangled wildly and weeping women crowded into the church, as though thinking to find sanctuary there. Others stood gazing helplessly up into the sky. Here I saw some Italian Infantry, mostly young, who were

[1] " Heave ! . . . Heave ! "

delighted to be retreating. " Forward, you militar-
ists ! " they cried to us as we passed. " This is your
punishment ! How much longer do you think the
war is going to last ? What about Trieste now ? "
They spoke with joyful irony, as though the conquest
of Trieste had been a slaves' task, imposed upon
unwilling Italy by foreign imperialists. They were
the only Italian troops I saw during the retreat, who
showed any sign of being under the influence of
" defeatist " or German propaganda.

The stream of refugees steadily thickened on the
roads. More than once I got down and ran on ahead,
calling out with monotonous refrain to the drivers of
civilian carts to keep well over to the right of the road,
so as to let the guns pass. They all did their best to
obey, poor brutes, and we gained some useful ground
in that endless column.

At nightfall we were still eight or nine kilometres
from Latisana. The traffic block grew worse and
worse, and there were too few Carabinieri to exercise
proper control. We stuck for hours at a time, with
nothing moving for miles, three motionless lines of
traffic abreast on the road, all pointing in the same
direction. Tired men slept and wakeful men waited
and watched and cursed at the delay. Behind us,
far off, we could hear the booming of the guns, which
seemed from hour to hour to come a little nearer,
and flashes of distant gunfire flickered in the night sky.
Back there the rear-guards were still fighting, and
brave men were dying to give us time to get away.
It seemed just then that their sacrifice might be in
vain. What a haul the Austrians would have here !

And behind and around us burning villages were still

flaming in the dark, and throwing up the sharp black outlines of the trees.

. . . . . .

Afterwards I heard of some of the deeds that had been done " back there." I heard of the charges of the Italian Cavalry, of the Novara Lancers and the Genoa Dragoons, crack regiments, full of the best horsemen in Italy, who had been waiting, waiting, all the war through, for their chance to come. Their chance had come at last, the chance to die, charging against overwhelming odds, in order that Italy, or at least the glory of her name, might live for ever. One commanding officer called all his officers around him and said, " The common people of Italy have betrayed our country's honour, and now we, the gentlemen of Italy, are going to save it ! " and then he led the charge, and fell leading it. It was a fine, aristocratic gesture, though the prejudices of his class partly blinded him.

Near Cervignano Italian Cavalry charged the massed machine guns of the enemy and, when the horses went down, the men went on, and then the men went down, all but a few, and those few for a moment broke the line and held up the advance, and gave to the mass of the retreating troops just that little space of extra time, which spans the gulf between escape and destruction.

And away up north on Monte Nero, left behind when the rest of the Army retired, Alpini and Bersaglieri resisted for many days, and aeroplanes flew back and dropped food and ammunition from the skies for them. And when their ammunition was all shot away, that garrison came down into the plains, and a

few survivors fought their way through with bombs
and bayonets back to the Italian lines.

And many other such deeds were surely done that
will never be known, because the men that did them
died out of sight of any of their comrades who survived.

.   .   .   .   .   .

In the small hours of the 30th of October, I left
our guns in Leary's charge and determined to walk
on to Latisana, to see if I could not find some person
in authority and get something done to move things on.
I had only gone a little way when I met Bixio, a
Captain of Mountain Artillery, attached to Raven's
Headquarters. He had come back to see how far
behind our rearmost guns were. I saw him several
times during the retreat. He did fine work more than
once in creating order out of confusion. He looked
a magnificent, almost a Mephistophelian, figure, with
his dark features, his flashing angry eyes, his air of
decision, his sharp gestures, his tall body enveloped
in a loose cloak, his Alpino hat, with its long single
feather. He told me that all traffic along this road
into Latisana had been stopped for the past three
hours, in order to let traffic from the north get on,
for it was from that direction that the advance of the
enemy was most threatening.

I walked on and found a British Red Cross Ambulance stuck in the block. I talked for a few moments
to the driver, who gave me a piece of cake and some
wine. When I reached Latisana, I found traffic
pouring through along the road from the north. I
crossed the bridge over the Tagliamento and looked
down at the broad swift current, glistening beneath.
Hope leapt again within me at the sight. Here,

at last, I said to myself, is a fine natural obstacle. We shall turn here and stand at bay, and the invader will come no further.

I had been told that there were some huts on the right hand side, just over the bridge, where our men would be, where the A.S.C. would have delivered rations and the Staff had fixed a rendezvous. I, therefore, expected to find the Major and our dismounted party, or at least someone from another Battery, or some of either Raven's or the General's Staff. But there was nothing there ; no British troops, no rations, and no Staff ! Only the never ending rain, and a confused stream of Italian troops, chiefly Field Guns, hurrying across the bridge.

There was nothing to do but to go back. The sentries on the bridge tried to stop me, but I insisted that I must see some Artillery officer in authority. They directed me to the Square, where I found Colonel Canale, controlling the movements of Batteries, looking straight before him out of uncomprehending, heavy eyes, like one crushed under a weight of bitter humiliation. He asked where our guns were. I told him they were getting near now, but stuck fast in the traffic. He said it was forbidden to let through traffic on that road at present, but he would do what he could. I asked if there were any new orders. " No," he said, " only forward across the bridge, and then push on as fast as possible to Portogruaro." I left him, and found three of our stragglers from the Major's party, asleep on the floor of a forge. I told them to cross the river and wait on the Portogruaro road for myself and the guns. I asked an Italian Corporal if there was anywhere in Latisana where one

could get a drink.   He said he thought not, but gave
me a bottle full of cold coffee, brandy and sugar in
about equal proportions.   It was a splendid drink,
but a little too sweet.

I walked back along the road towards the guns.
Some houses on the outskirts of the town were burning
furiously.   The traffic was beginning to move forward
along our road, very slowly and with frequent halts.
I had two overcoats with me when we started from
Pec.   Both were long ago wet through, and I was
wearing over my shoulders at this time a blanket lent
to me by Medola.   This, too, was thoroughly drenched
by now.   In the fields on either side of the road
Infantry were lying out in the rain, asleep, dreaming,
perhaps, of Rome or Sicily or the Bay of Naples.   The
dawn of another day was breaking, cold, damp and
miserable, symbolic of this great weary tragedy.

.   .   .   .   .   .

I had not gone far when I met four of our men
carrying on a stretcher the dead body of the Battery
Staff Sergeant Artificer.   He had dropped asleep
on one of the guns and, as the tractor moved on, he
had fallen forward, head downwards, beneath the gun
wheel, which had passed over him, along the whole
length of his body, crushing him to death.   They
said he died before they could get him out.   He was
a good man and a very skilled worker, full of pluck
and spirit.   The last thing he had done for me was
to get everything ready for rendering the guns un-
serviceable in case we should have to abandon them.
There was no chance of decent burial for him here,
but I had his body placed upon an empty trench cart,
which was being towed by a lorry of another Battery,

and put two of our men in charge of it. They buried him the next day or the day after in a cemetery near Portogruaro.

About 7 a.m., as I was still making my way back through the traffic towards our guns, it was reported that enemy cavalry patrols had been seen to the north of the road, and that shots had been exchanged. For a moment there was some panic and confusion, but a scheme of defence was quickly organised. No one had supposed that they could yet be so near. I found Bixio rallying some Infantrymen, with eloquent words and great gestures, and an Italian Infantry Major, calm and smiling, was putting out a screen of machine gunners and riflemen across the road itself and along a hedge five hundred yards to the north of it. All was in readiness for putting our guns completely out of action. There would be nothing else to do, if the enemy appeared, for we had no gun ammunition, and it was impossible to get on, until the whole traffic block in front of us had been shifted forward. But I told Bixio that I should do nothing to the guns, unless there was some evidence that the enemy was really approaching with a superiority of force over our own.

The enemy, however, did not at that time reappear and the best bit of hustling traffic management that I had yet witnessed during the retreat, now took place. The northern road was at last clear at Latisana, and the authorities turned their attention to us. A breakdown gang appeared and a number of new tractors and lorries with refills of petrol. Civilian carts whose drivers remained, were ordered to drive on, those which had been abandoned were overturned

to one side into the ditches, and dead horses and
wreckage due to bombing or the brief moments of
panic were likewise thrust off the road. Relays of
fresh drivers took over all the lorries and tractors
which would still go. The rest went into the ditch
on top of the dead horses and derelict carts. The
heavier loads which single tractors had been pulling
were split up between two or more. In a surprisingly
short time the whole mass began to move.

Here I parted from Medola, who had been a very
good friend to us. Our three guns got a new tractor
to themselves and I got up beside the driver. And
so at last we entered Latisana. Our new driver was
immensely enthusiastic, but very excited. He told
me that he had had two brothers killed in the war and
had applied, when the retreat began, to be transferred
from Mechanical Transport to the Infantry. That
morning, he said, he had heard General Pettiti, who
was our Army Corps Commander, give the order that
all the British Batteries must first be got across the
river and only then the Italian. I said that I saw
no good reason for this preference, but that anyhow
he was driving the last three British guns. This
pleased him tremendously. By now I was wrapped
up in a new and dry Italian blanket, which I had taken
from an abandoned cart by the roadside.

Our tractor, less enthusiastic than its driver, broke
down continually. It was rumoured that the bridge
had been blown up already, and there were wild screams
of despair from a crowd of women, who came running
past us. At last we turned the last corner and came
in sight of the Tagliamento. The bridge was still
intact. Italian Generals were rushing to and fro,

gesticulating, giving orders. General Pettiti sent a special orderly to ask me if mine were the last British guns. I told him yes. Our tractor broke down three times on the bridge itself. But at last we were over. One of our party had an Italian flag and waved it and cried " Viva l'Italia ! " Not long after, the bridge went up, with an explosion that could be heard for miles around.

CHAPTER XXIII

FROM THE TAGLIAMENTO TO TREVISO

I HEARD later that the Major and his party had reached Latisana the previous day. Winterton had joined them near Muzzano. They had marched for forty-eight hours practically without food and with only some three hours' rest in stray halts. They had been magnificent, but they were utterly done, and the Major, who had been most done of all, told me afterwards that it had made him cry to watch them hobbling along,—some of them men too old or of too low a medical category to have passed for the Infantry,—and to hear them singing,

> " What's the use of worrying ?
> It never was worth while.
> So pack up your sorrows in your old kit bag,
> And smile, smile, smile ! "

The spirit of the men in the retreat from Mons was not finer than the spirit of those men of ours.

9

At Latisana they got on board a train for Treviso.
It was about the last train that was running.

.   .   .   .   .   .

My party, though they were longer on the road,
were at least able to ride a great part of the way on
the tractors and guns.

Once across the Tagliamento, our tractor not only
continued to break down every few hundred yards,
but also developed the unpleasant habit of catching
fire. Twice we put the fire out with the squirts and
chemicals provided for the purpose, and a third time
with mud. I determined not to risk a fourth time,
and so pulled on to the side of the road and halted.
I sent on the Battery Sergeant Major on a passing
lorry to Portogruaro with a note to the Major asking
that another tractor might be sent back, and I also
sent Avoglia to the nearest Italian Headquarters to
see if he could raise a tractor there. We were halted
at the top of a hill on the road running along the
western bank of the river. We were indeed literally
" across," but we should have provided a splendid
target for enemy Artillery advancing on the further
side. A good system of trenches ran alongside the
road, and these were now manned in force by Italian
Infantry. Field Guns also had come into position
behind them. Our men took advantage of the
enforced halt to collect fuel, light fires and make tea.
We were still halted here at nightfall.

Soon after dark some Italians came up and told us
that we were blocking the road, which was not true,
as we were well to the side. However, as neither
Avoglia nor the Sergeant Major had yet returned
with a new tractor, and as the Italians said that they

would pull us on, I cordially agreed to the attempt being made. They attached a tractor with a heavy lorry in tow to our inflammatory tractor and our three guns. They asked that an attempt should be made to start up our tractor also, but I succeeded in persuading them that this was inexpedient. They then started up their own tractor only. To my great surprise, we began to move. It was a magnificent machine, and forged ahead splendidly, contrary to all the laws limiting its capacity, rumbling and back-firing under the unwonted strain, for miles through the gloom.

Then the moon began to rise. The night, for the first time since the retreat began, was fine and clear. We could only go slowly and broke down now and then. But all went pretty well, until we swung our long train a little too sharply round a corner in the road, and the last two guns got ditched. While we were trying to get them out, a British Major, whom I will call Star, appeared on the scene. He came from Portogruaro with the news that five new tractors were on their way back, and that some other British guns were ditched further ahead. I therefore thanked the officer in charge of the Italian tractor and lorry for all he had done for us and advised him now to go on and leave us, as our position was tiresome but no longer critical. This he did.

The moonlight was now bright as day, and one of Star's promised tractors arrived and finally succeeded in getting out our ditched guns.

.   .   .   .   .   .

Star had painted a bright picture of Portogruaro. All the British guns, he said, were parked together

in the Piazza and there was a large granary close by,
full of happy men with plenty of rations and straw.
So, it seems, some imaginative person had told him.
We reached Portogruaro in the small hours of the
31st of October. The moon had set and it was very
dark. Several of us made a most careful search in
the Piazza. But there were no British guns there, no
granary, no straw, no rations. I halted the guns just
outside the gate of the town and told the men to turn
in and sleep. Soon after daybreak we all woke feeling
very hungry. I issued practically all that remained
of our rations, a little bully, a little biscuit and a
very little tea.

Wanting a wash and, still more urgently, a shave,
I went into a house and asked for the loan of some
soap and a towel. A number of terrified old women
gathered round me, in doubt whether to fly or to stay.
I advised them to stay, for I took for granted at this
time that the Tagliamento line would hold. They
pressed upon me coffee and bread, and I heard them
repeating over and over again to one another my
assurances that the enemy was still far away and
would never get as far as Portogruaro. It was hard
not to cry.

Star arrived during the morning and took charge.
There was no need, he said, to hurry on. We had
better rest here for a day. He arranged for us all to
draw rations from the Italian Comando di Tappa.
Treviso was to be our next stopping place. We
were disturbed a little during the morning by enemy
planes dropping bombs on the town, but none fell very
near us.

In the afternoon we moved on and parked our guns

near the station along with those of the other British
Batteries, which had arrived before us. Bombing
raids continued and were more serious that afternoon
than in the morning. One bomb fell on a house, which
was full of men from one of the other Batteries, and
caused a number of casualties. It was only by good
luck that a number of my own men were not in that
house at the time. Fortunately I had had words,
as two tired men will, with one of the officers of the
other Battery, about the joint use of the kitchen, and
my men, when I asked them, had decided that they
preferred, as always, to " run their own show " and
not " pig in with other Batteries." To that attitude of
independence some of them probably owe their lives.

In the afternoon Raven turned up, and said that he
had arranged for us to go on to Treviso by train.
We loaded our guns on to trucks, and waited several
hours in the station yard for the promised train.
It was cold and wet and more bombers came over us.
They had bombed the station for the last three nights,
I heard. But nothing hit it while we were there. The
train left at 9.30 p.m. Leary and another officer and
I tried to share one wet blanket. We were too wet
and cold to sleep. I walked up and down the carriage
trying to get warm. They bombed the railway several
times during our journey, and once, when a bomb
fell near our train, there was a rumour that the engine
driver had gone away and left us standing. But it
was quite untrue. We crawled along, with many
stops. It seemed a quite interminable journey.
But at 8 o'clock next morning, the 1st of November,
we came to Treviso.

CHAPTER XXIV

THOUGHTS AFTER THE DISASTER

WE hung about for a while in the station, nobody knowing what was to happen next. Then Leary and I went off to try to find some food. We had been living just lately on ration biscuits and a tin of Australian peach jam. There was not much left at the Buffet, where we found Bixio, but we got a little salami and some eels and wine and coffee. Meanwhile our train had gone on to Mestre, owing to a mistake between two railway officials, and had to return next day. Leary's feet were so bad that he could hardly walk. I got them dressed for him by the Italian Red Cross, but he could walk no better afterwards. The Villa Passi, the British Headquarters, was several miles off. An enemy plane came over and bombed Treviso, when we were in the station square, trying in vain to find a conveyance. But none of the bombs fell very close to us. At last we hailed a British lorry, which took us to Villa Passi, and then on to Carbonera, where odds and ends of Batteries had been turning up for several days past. The Major was very delighted to see us, a rumour having got about that we and the last guns had been left on the wrong side of the Tagliamento, when the bridge went up. He had almost given up hope of seeing us again.

Then I went to bed and slept for hours and hours. Next morning from my window I could see the Alps lying very low on the horizon, like a ball of fluffy snow. The sun was shining and a fountain was playing in the garden. I could hardly realise that we had reached, for a moment at least, a place of peace, where there was no more fighting or retreating. Our men were worn out, most of them, and slept like logs. They had been sorely tried. Their pluck and endurance had been splendid. But they got no message of thanks or praise from the British General who at that time nominally commanded us. This distinguished man I had last seen in the Square at Palmanova, amid the smoke and flames, with his car standing close at hand ready to push off, and he had arrived at Treviso in good time. He was now comfortably installed at the Villa Passi, and the day some of our footsore men limped into Treviso, he was lunching with his Staff, all bright and polished and sleek, in the Hotel Stella d'Oro.

We all expected, for days, that he would call a parade and address the men who had saved what he used to call " his guns," or at least that he would send some message. But he made no sign, except to open a canteen for the sale of the 20,000 cigarettes, which some intelligent subordinate had saved in preference to valuable gun stores now in Austrian hands.

.　　.　　.　　.　　.　　.

The day after my arrival I read a newspaper for the first time for over a week, but the news was very bad and the retreat still continuing. The Austrians were across the Tagliamento in strong force at several points. I tried to reason and make distinctions, but my brain was still too tired to answer the helm, so I left it. We ate hot polenta and drank wonderful coffee, having established our Battery Mess in the porter's lodge at the entrance to the Villa Lebreton, and persuaded the porter's wife to cook for us. All the Battery had discovered the polenta at the porter's lodge and our men crowded the kitchen at all hours of the day. We all appreciated good food after the short rations of the retreat.

Conversation was intensely depressing when not utterly trivial. I remember walking round and round the vegetable garden at the back of the Villa with an Italian friend of mine, trying both to face the facts and to draw some comfort from them. It was an impossible task. My friend was full of despair and bitterness. "The fruits of thirty months of war all lost in two days," he said, "and much more lost besides! What will all the mothers think, who have lost sons on San Michele and Monte Santo? It is a common thing in Italy now for families to have lost four or five sons. What will the mothers of Italy think of this? Would not any of them be justified in shooting Cadorna? The Third Army should not have been ordered to retire. They should have counter-attacked instead. But now would it not be better to make peace at once? Is there no man who will rise up and say, 'Stop, stop, stop this bloody business now, before it gets any worse?' Some of our soldiers looked quite pleased to be retreating. Poor children! They thought the war was over and they were going home. There is a frightful danger that the leaders,—the generals and the politicians at Rome,—will say 'fight on!' but the rank and file will go on breaking. 'We are fighting for Trento and Trieste!' they used to say, and now they say 'we are organising the defence of the Piave line!' The

Regular soldiers never want the war to end. And soon they will be distributing medals for the retreat. Medals ! ''

I could find no words worth saying to him in reply. '' What will they be saying about us now in London and Paris ? '' he went on. '' They will be saying,'' I replied, '' that help must be sent to you,'' but my answer I know sounded flat and empty. '' Yes,'' he said bitterly, '' perhaps *now* you will send some of your generals and your troops to Italy. And so you will put us under orders and under obligations to you, and we shall become your slaves. Italians are used to being looked upon as the slaves of other nations.'' '' No,'' I said, '' all that is over. Those of us who know the facts, know what Italy has done and suffered for the Alliance in this war. It will not be forgotten. Moments of supreme crisis such as this test the value and the depth of an Alliance. And ours will stand the test.''

But that day he was inconsolable. For Italy was wounded and bleeding, and the dramatic swiftness and horror of the disaster had bent her pride and almost broken it. But, though the future seemed black as a night without stars, the hope of a coming daybreak remained strong in the hearts of a few. But the struggle ahead would be cruelly hard. What had Italy left to offer those who would still fight in her defence ? Still, as of old,

> '' Only her bosom to die on,
> Only her heart for a home,
> And a name with her children to be,
> From Calabrian to Adrian Sea,
> Mother of cities made free.''

Yet this was a rich reward when, a year later, the
dawn broke in all its glory.

.   .   .   .   .

I turned over and over in my mind in the weeks and
months that followed, as fresh evidence accumulated,
the meaning and the causes of the disaster of Caporetto,
and gradually I came to definite and clear cut conclusions.   It was the Second Army that had been
broken, and in the course of the retreat had almost
disappeared.   It was a common thing to hear the
Second Army spoken of as a whole Army of cowards
and " defeatists."   Many foreign critics, with minds
blankly ignorant of nearly all the facts, seemed to
think that the whole business could be accounted for
by a few glib phrases about German and Socialist
propaganda, or the supposed lack of fighting qualities
in the Italian race.   Yet it was this same Second
Army, which in those now distant days in August
had conquered the Bainsizza Plateau, amid the
acclamations of all the Allied world.   Whole Armies
do not change their nature in a night, even when
worn out with fighting and heavy casualties.   The
thing was not so simple as that.

.   .   .   .   .   .

In fixing responsibility for Caporetto, one must
draw a sharp distinction between responsibility for
the original break in a narrow sector of the line, and
responsibility for not making good that break, before
the situation had got hopelessly out of hand.   In
the former case the responsibility must rest partly upon
the troops and subordinate Staff charged with holding
that narrow sector and partly upon the High
Command ; in the latter case the chief responsibility,

and a far graver one, must rest upon the dispositions of the High Command. This was the view apparently taken by the Commission appointed by the Italian Government to investigate the whole question, for the three chief Generals concerned were not only removed from their commands, but given no further employment and placed upon half-pay.

The original break was due to many causes. The great mass of German Divisions and Artillery was concentrated in the Caporetto sector. This fact should have been known to the High Command, and if the Italian troops holding the line at this point were, for various reasons, of poor quality, this also should have been known to the High Command, whose duty it is to know the comparative fighting power of different units. The High Command, when the battle started, claimed that they had known beforehand when and where the blow was coming, that all preparations had been made and that they were fully confident of the result. Such boasts have been made by other High Commands on other Fronts, on the eve of other disasters, and even after them. They greatly deepen the responsibility of those who make them.

The German Batteries on the Italian Front had a much larger supply of ammunition than the Austrians, including a large quantity of " special gas " shell. Many Italian troops, both Infantry and Artillery, subjected to prolonged gas bombardment, found the gas masks provided by the High Command quite inadequate. It was left for General Diaz some months later to order the equipment of the whole Italian Army with the British box respirator.

The number of guns lost by the Second Army was

very great. I am told that one reason for this was
the fact that the High Command had for some weeks
been preparing a further big offensive against the
Plateau of Ternova, had concentrated an abnormal
number of Batteries on the Second Army Front, and
had pushed the majority of the guns much further up
than would have been justified, if an enemy offensive
had been expected. Then, having made these preparations, the High Command hesitated and began
to change its mind. But the disposition of the forward
Batteries, thoroughly unsound for defensive purposes,
was not appreciably altered, and a quite small enemy
advance sufficed to make enormous captures of guns.

When the attack developed, some of the troops in
the Caporetto sector unquestionably turned and ran,
as troops of every great Army in this war have at times
turned and run, under conditions of greater or less
provocation. Then the High Command apparently
lost its head, and attempted to issue to the world a
communiqué of a character unparalleled in the history
of this war, naming and cursing, as traitors to their
country, certain particular Infantry Brigades. This
document was very properly suppressed by the
Italian Government.

But where were the reserves which the High Command should have had ready to repair the broken
line ? And where were the plans for retreating to
prepared positions only a short distance behind ?
It was well known, and indeed it used to be another
boast of the High Command, that a local reverse
would be of no great importance, seeing that there
were no less than twelve prepared lines between the
Front, as it then ran, and Udine. I have seen some

of those lines with my own eyes. I know what great and patient labour went to the making of them, and I know how strong they were. But, when the moment came to make use of them, no one outside the charmed circle of the High Command was in possession of the plans for their defence, and for falling back upon them in an orderly and systematic manner. It has been said that these plans could not have been made known beforehand to the Subordinate Commands for fear they should fall into the hands of spies. That would have been a small misfortune compared to what actually befell.[1]

When, owing to the omissions of the High Command, the break in the line was swiftly widened and the whole defensive scheme of the Second Army collapsed, it is true that confusion and panic began to spread through the Second Army like fire through dry grass. But it is not within the power of common soldiers, and especially of simple unlettered peasantry, such as most of these soldiers were, to repair the blunders of bad Staff work, and to make for themselves, on the spur of the moment and in face of deadly peril, plans which trained brains should have elaborated long before, at leisure and in safe secluded places. When leadership fails, the best troops fail too. But let one who comes of a nation, none of whose troops have ever acted as those troops of the Italian Second Army acted in those dreadful days, throw the first stone at Italy.

---

[1] In fairness to General Capello, the Second Army Commander, who had been highly and deservedly praised for the Bainsizza victory in August, and who was one of the generals removed from his command after Caporetto, it should be stated that on the latter occasion he was away from the Front on leave.

That nation will be hard to find. It is not of this world.

Those who know the Italian soldier know that no soldier in the world responds more readily to loyal trust, to common kindliness and to efficient and inspiring leadership. British and French officers, who have had opportunities of judging, know this as well as Italians. But the Italian High Command denied these things to the Italian soldier.[1] It is due to him and to the good name of Italy, which has been damnably traduced by prejudiced and ignorant men, that the truth should be spoken,

The dark and tragic story of the Italian retreat is lit up by many deeds of heroism, wherein the Italian soldier showed all his accustomed valour. And it was only by the valour of the Italian soldier that the retreat was stayed on the Piave line, which the High Command pronounced to be untenable and wished to abandon, but which the Cabinet at Rome, pinning their faith to the qualities of the Italian soldier rather than to the opinions of the High Command, ordered to be held at all hazards. And the Cabinet at Rome was right. The Italian line stiffened and stood upon the Piave, while the Allied reinforcements were still on the further side of the Alps. If

[1] Among other charges which may be brought against the High Command at this time are, first, their failure to make adequate provision for the amusement and relaxation of the troops when in rest, such as the Y.M.C.A. and various concert parties provided for British troops, to combat inevitable war-weariness ; second, failure to increase the most inadequate scale of rations ; and, third, the attempt to apply, with strange disregard of the very different spirit of the Italian people, some of the worst and most brutal traditions of German discipline. All this was altered later by General Diaz and the Orlando Ministry.

only Lloyd George and Bissolati had had their way, and these reinforcements had been sent a few months earlier, if only we had been able to put a British Army Corps, with its full complement of aircraft, guns and shells, against the Hermada, if only we had had half a dozen tanks to send down the Vippacco Valley, what a different story there would have been to tell !

* * * * * *

We ourselves were out of the first stages of that great defence. We had no ammunition, and we were terribly short of gun stores, though the bare guns had all been saved. And our men were very short of steel helmets and box respirators, and the boots and clothing of many were in a pitiful condition. But a small supply of ammunition came through from France, and it was decided to send one Section of the Battery into action on the Piave and the remainder back to Ferrara to refit. All gun stores and men's equipment were to be pooled, and those going back were to be stripped for the benefit of those going forward. I remember very vividly our Battery parade on the morning of the 4th of November, when we had to take from some men their greatcoats and even their caps, tunics and boots, in order to make up some sort of equipment for the Right Section which was going forward with the Major. I was put in command of the Left Section, stripped bare for its journey to Ferrara.

The evening before our departure I walked up and down the avenue outside our Villa and talked with Venosta, who had done splendid work in the retreat. He had heard from the survivors of a Cavalry Regiment, who had passed back along the road an hour before, that a Turkish Division was in Udine, and Turkish cavalry in Palmanova. Bulgarians also were said to be on this Front, raping, after Serbs, Greeks and Rumanians, Italians also. It was said that Turks had been on Faiti and Volconiac at the end. I had no sure evidence of this, but, if it was true, the Turks' notorious incapacity for an offensive would help to explain our surprising escape. What we had needed, all through the days of the retreat, was enough rain to swell the rivers and make heavy the roads. What we had got, after the first three days, was brilliant sunshine. The stars in their courses seemed to be fighting against Italy. " Dio uno ed unno ! " said one Italian bitterly.

CHAPTER XXV

FERRARA, ARQUATA AND THE CORNICE ROAD

WE reached Ferrara at 5 a.m. and drove in lorries from the railway station past the Castello of the d'Estes to the Palestro Barracks, the Depôt of the 14th Regiment of Italian Field Artillery. Here we were to be lodged by the Italian military authorities. We were received with every consideration and great hospitality. Our men had excellent quarters in the Barracks. Our officers were invited to have their meals in the Italian Artillery officers' Mess, which was a large and comfortable place and where the food was not only good, but very much cheaper than could have been got outside. The Colonel also offered to put riding horses at the disposal of any of us who should care to ride. I was much struck by the sensible lack of ceremony of this Italian Mess, by comparison with similar Depôt Messes in our own Army. There was no waiting in the anteroom for senior officers who were late, no asking permission of senior officers to leave the table early. Within the hours fixed for meals everyone came in and out as they pleased. There was no special table for the Staff, no rule against bringing evening papers into dinner, no aloofness, no pomposity. The only un-English formalities were the habit of turning and bowing as one left the Mess, if a number of officers were still present, and the universal Italian custom by which a newcomer at his first appearance would walk round and shake hands in turn with all those whom he did not know and introduce himself to them by name.

We·were also invited to become members during our stay of the Circolo Negozianti, or Merchants' Club, of Ferrara. This Club had spacious premises in an old Palazzo, and was the warmest place in the town, having a most efficient system of central heating.

Ferrara is spread over a large area relatively to its population ; it has broad streets and very few slums. But it has come down in the world since the Renaissance. Degenerate descendants of the d'Estes of that time stripped many of the Palazzi of their artistic beauties and sold them to help pay their debts. Ferrara is a city of old Palazzi, street after street of them, inhabited mainly now by well-to-do peasants, who take a pride in keeping up their exteriors. One

of the most interesting sights in the city is the Palazzo
Schifanoia, now used as a museum and containing
frescoes by Cossa and Cosimo Tura. But what most
appealed to me was the superb western façade of the
Cathedral.

In peace time Ferrara is prosperous, though a little
isolated from the main currents of Italian life. It
is the chief centre of food distribution for this part
of the country, and is well known for its bakeries.
It is also an important centre for the hemp export
trade.

After two days at Ferrara I was chosen to go to
Arquata Scrivia, a little town on the main line north
of Genoa. This had been selected as the Base for
the British Forces in Italy, and I was to get in touch
with the Ordnance people there, to give them a list
of our really urgent requirements and try to hasten
their delivery, so as to get us back into action as soon
as possible. Siramo, an Italian Artillery officer who
was attached to us for *liaison*, accompanied me.

The ordinary passenger train for Bologna was
three and a half hours late. Special trains were
coming through every ten minutes from Treviso and
Venice packed with refugees, going southwards.
The organisation of the Italian railways at this time
for clearing the refugees from the fighting zone was
exceedingly good. Siramo thought that, if Venice
had to be abandoned, the Germans and Austrians
would not damage it. I felt no such security. That
night we stopped at Milan. Wild stories of " tradi-
mento " were in the air. It was being said, for
instance, that two Generals of the Second Army had
been marched through their troops in handcuffs

under a guard of Carabinieri. It was also officially announced that Diaz had replaced Cadorna in command of the Italian Armies.

Next day we reached Arquata amid the tumble of the Ligurian Hills, whose sides were clothed with chestnuts and oaks and vine terraces. We found British Staff, Sanitary Sections and Ordnance already in possession. The Ordnance were occupying a large villa just outside the town. My old friend Shield, whom I had known at Palmanova, was there, but most of the others were new arrivals from France. They were surprisingly full of cheerfulness, as *imboscati* are often apt to be, even when things are going badly at the Front. The Italian disaster evidently meant very little to them ; they hardly realised it at all. They were the first cheerful people I had seen since the retreat began, and it was no doubt good for Siramo and myself to be cheered up. But it grated on both of us a little.

At my first interview I got the impression that the Ordnance were surprisingly efficient and would be very prompt in giving us what we wanted. But I gradually discovered that they really possessed very little of what they first promised me, and that nothing was known for certain as to when further stores would arrive. I telephoned to Ferrara that the immediate prospects were poor, and was told in reply to wait three or four days and see how much turned up. Having pestered various Ordnance officers to the limit of their endurance, I therefore decided to go away for two days.

Siramo went for two days to his family at Turin and I took the train to Genoa, arriving in the early

afternoon. After lunch I set out to walk eastwards
along the Cornice Road. It was a relief to my thoughts
and feelings to be quite alone. The day was windy
and sunless and rather cold, but the warm and
audacious colouring of the Villas and the little fishing
villages seemed almost to draw sunshine out of the
dull sky. I stopped at Sturla and drank two cups
of coffee and ate some biscuits, and decided to walk
on to Nervi. It was now near the hour of sunset
and the sun, having kept invisible all day, half broke
through the clouds, turning them first red and then
golden. So the sky was when I came to Quarto dei
Mille, with its monument looking out to sea, that
historic place whence Garibaldi and the Thousand
set sail for their great adventure, the liberation of
Sicily and Naples, and the unification of Italy, with
British warships following them, some say by chance,
so that the enemies of Italy dared not interrupt their
passage.

Then said I to myself, standing all alone at Quarto,
"Italy will not be defeated, nor even mainly saved
from defeat by foreign aid. The strongest and best
of her children will pull her through, even though
they be not all the nation. But the rest will do their
share also, and will follow, when the bravest lead.
How young, and how uncertain of herself as yet, is
Italy! And yet, how lovable, how well worth
serving!"   The Germans with their "special gas"
and with other factors in their favour, counted on
breaking, not only the line of the Second Army, but
the morale of the Italian people. For a moment
they seemed to have succeeded. In the darkest days
I talked with many whose stuffing seemed all gone.

But then, with the promise of Allied help, with the sight of even a handful of new French and British uniforms, and under the spell of the oratory of their statesmen and their journalists, things began to change and Italian hearts grew brave again.

The Italians are a mercurial people. If they are more easily cast down by defeat than we British, they are more easily encouraged by even the distant prospect of victory, and they react to influences that would leave us unmoved. The coarse insults of the enemy press were everywhere angrily quoted, and the national spirit rose to a red glow of passion. The Socialists Turati and Treves,—the latter the author of the famous phrase, " nessuno in trincee quest' inverno," [1]—who before Caporetto had criticised the war as aggressive, imperialist and unnecessary, said now that all Italians must unite and fight on to drive back the invader from Italian soil. And cool brains, such as Nitti and Einaudi, reinforced all this with logical demonstrations of the economic impossibility of a separate peace, with the enemy Powers strained to the utmost by the blockade and Italy dependent on the Allies for shipping, food and coal. The Germans would have done far more wisely, if, instead of attacking, they had aimed only at holding the Italian Army along its old line.

I walked on from Quarto to Nervi and, as it was getting dark, I decided to take a tram for the last few kilometres. But all the trams were standing still, the current having been switched off for several hours. So I stood on the step of a tram and talked to the conductor about the war, and tried to cheer

[1] " No one in the trenches this winter."

him up by telling him that the Germans were on their
last legs, and were making their last great effort,
and that the Allies had only to hold together a little
longer, and throw sufficient force against the enemy
here in Italy, in order to see a far bigger and more
precipitate and disastrous retreat than Caporetto,
and next time in the other direction. All this I not
only said, but firmly believed (and it all came true
within a year). At first he was very despondent,
but he warmed up as I proceeded, and began to
gesticulate again and regain animation and compli-
ment me on my Italian. And then the current also
was restored, and the tram moved on, and we came
to Nervi, where I dined well and slept at the Albergo
Cristoforo Colombo. I am not in general an admirer
of palm trees, but they are sometimes impressive in
the dusk, towering over one's head, as they do at
Nèrvi, in the long mixed avenue of palms and orange
trees which leads down to the station from the town.

Next morning I got up early and walked back
towards Genoa along the Via Marina. The sun was
shining on the sea and the dark rocks, the stone pines
and the great aloes and the brightly coloured villas.
There was an exhilaration in the air and I was in
the midst of beauty, and, for the first time for many
days, I was for a little while really happy. Later
on I took a tram back to Genoa, and walked up to
the tall lighthouse on the further side of the town,
and looked westward at the great curve of the shore,
beyond the breakwater and the sands.

In some of the stations along the line were placards,
" Long live great old England," " Welcome to the
valiant British Army," " Vive la France," " Vive la

victorieuse Armée de Verdun." The first of the Allied reinforcements were arriving.

At Arquata station I met an advance party of the Northumberland Fusiliers. They told me that they had been quite moved by their wonderful welcome on the way through Italy and by all the hospitality shown to their officers and men at the stations where they had stopped. It gave me a queer thrill to see British Infantrymen again after many months, and this time on Italian soil.

．　　．　　．　　．　　．　　．

After various orders and counter-orders I left Arquata for Ferrara on the 16th, with two truckloads of stores. But this was only a very small proportion of the minimum which we required.

CHAPTER XXVI

REFITTING AT FERRARA

I GOT back to Ferrara on the evening of November 17th, and shared a bedroom with Jeune, who had returned from leave in England, having missed all our most unpleasant experiences. Our brother officers of the Italian Field Artillery were very hospitable and courteous to us through those weeks of waiting. We could do nothing till the Ordnance sent us gun stores from Arquata, and these dribbled in very slowly, a few odds and ends at a time.

I often went out riding on the Piazza d'Arme and

along the ramparts and in the country round Ferrara
with Italian officers.   Days were still very anxious,
and the news from the Front not always good, and
one rather avoided talking about the war.   But one
evening at dinner I succeeded in piercing the polite
reserve of a little Captain who was sitting next to me.
" Italy should have made it a condition of her intervention," he said, " that the other Allies should
have sent troops to the Italian Front.   Also more
guns and war material.   Italy, at the beginning of
her war, had many heroes but few guns.   The other
Allies, equally with Italy, are without statesmen.
Your Lloyd George is energetic, but——!   The
British are not really at war with Austria.   They
have soft sentiments towards her and don't want her
to lose too much.   The Jugo-Slav propaganda was
at its height, and was being encouraged in Paris and
London, at the very moment when Italy was being
pressed by the French and British to enter the war.

"We have made too many offensives on our
own, unaided.   Cadorna should have refused, but
he went on and on.   He sacrificed thousands of lives
uselessly.   He demanded too much of his troops.   He
did not understand them.   This last disaster was
caused by Croats and Bulgarians, who spoke Italian
perfectly, having lived among us and taken degrees
at our Universities, getting through our lines in the
first confusion, dressed in Italian uniform, and
sending false telephone messages and signals in our
own cipher, ordering a general retreat.[1]   It was men

---

[1] I heard this story many times and I believe this was one of
the causes of the rapid increase of the first confusion.   The
Austrians had tried this trick without success against the Third

from ——,[1] who first ran away at Rombon and Tolmino. It has been often proved in the history of our country that those men have no courage. Italians have too little unity."

He went on to speak of economic difficulties. " Italy is poor," he said, " and the Allies are rich. Yet coal costs four times as much in Italy as in France, and shipping is hardly to be had. Our Government has never driven hard enough bargains with the other Allies. After all, Italy came into the war as a volunteer, and not under the conscription of old treaties. But the Allies give her no credit for this. The French, since the war began, have recovered all their old ' blague.' They talk incessantly of what they have done, and despise everyone else. But look how unstable they are politically! They change their ministries, as often as some men change their mistresses. The Pope, too, is an enemy of Italy and a friend of Austria. He aims at the restoration of his temporal power. Many of the priests went about, both before and after Caporetto, trying to betray their country. Some told the soldiers that God had sent the disaster of Caporetto to show them the folly and the sinfulness of loving their corruptible country here below in poor earthly Italy, better than the incorruptible country of all good Catholics, God's eternal kingdom in the skies ! "

He spoke bitterly, as was not unnatural.

I made the acquaintance also in the Mess of a

Army on the Carso, as had the Germans against us in France. There must obviously be a certain amount of confusion already existing, if the trick is to have any chance of succeeding.

[1] A certain province in Italy, not his own.

Medical Officer, named Rossi, in peace time a University Professor of Nervous Pathology, who was now in charge of a hospital for " nervosi," or shell-shock cases, four miles outside the town. One afternoon Jeune and I accepted an invitation to visit this hospital. We drove out to it in a carrozza, accompanied by Rossi and a young woman, who went there daily to teach some of the illiterate patients to read and write.

No one can begin to understand what modern war means without some personal acquaintance with shell-shock cases. They are, especially for non-combatants, the most instructive of all the fruits of war, much more instructive than dead bodies or men without limbs. And then, having watched and talked or tried to talk with a variety of these still living creatures, let any man, even a profiteer or a theologian, look into his heart and ask himself whether he really agrees with the Chaplain, whom I have already quoted, that " three or four years of war may be tremendously worth while."

It needs a greater pen than mine to do justice to all we saw that afternoon, for we went through all the wards and saw all the sights there were to see. We saw a young Lieutenant, with large staring eyes, sitting up in bed. When we approached him, he jumped round in his bed very violently, as though his body had been shot out of a gun, and went on staring at us, speechless and with eyes full of wild terror. We saw two soldiers in the corner of a ward, their heads wobbling in perfect rhythm, ceaselessly from side to side, like the pendulum of a clock, with dead expressionless faces. We saw men cowering

beneath their bed clothes, trembling with an endless
terror. We saw a man who for months had quite
lost his speech, and was now just able to whisper,
almost inaudibly, " papa '" and " mama," a middle-
aged man with a beard. We saw a man with frightened
eyes, like a child in a nightmare, with many of the
outward signs of having been gassed, struggling
for breath, gesticulating feebly, trying to ward off
some imaginary blow. He had not been gassed,
but wounded in the head. He was alone in a blue
ward, where all our faces looked yellow. We saw
a youth lying asleep, white as a sheet and with hardly
any flesh left on his bones. He had been asleep for
two months without ever waking. We saw a splendid,
tall, bearded man, a Cavalry Captain, with a deep
voice and a firm handgrip, who could realise the
present, but had forgotten all the past. We saw a
multitude of minor " tremblers," and men undergoing
electrical treatment for paralysis and stiffness of
various limbs. One little man, another University
Professor, who was almost paralysed in both legs,
tried to advance to meet us and nearly fell forward
on the ground at our feet. I spoke also to a young
man with a paralysed back and left arm. I said I
hoped he would soon be better. " Yes," he said,
" I hope soon to go back to the Front." For a
moment I thought this was irony addressed to a
countryman of Mr Lloyd George. But it wasn't. He
really meant it. We went into the Convalescents'
Mess. There were about twenty present, smiling
and very gentle and quiet, like men who were not
yet quite sure of the world. One elderly man, a
Medical Captain, said to me, very softly, that it was a

great pleasure to see visitors from the outside, " especially our Allies."   At that moment I could easily have
wept.   Such sights as I had seen did not physically
sicken, nor even much horrify, me.   They just
tautened all my nerves and made me feel that all
my questions were impertinent, and all my good
wishes flat and empty, and that I resembled a visitor
to a Zoo.

On the way back to Ferrara we talked of literature
and Rossi, basing himself chiefly on Wells and Kipling,
said that the English, judged by their modern writers,
seemed to be a race " logical, but a little isolated."

Two days later the Major and the Right Section
of the Battery came to Ferrara, being replaced on the
Piave by a section of another Battery.   On the 1st
of December British Infantry, belonging to the XIVth
Corps, moved into the lines for the first time, taking
over the Montello sector, to the south of the Italian
Fourth Army.   This sector was to be held by British
troops for four months, but it is worth while again
to emphasise the fact that nearly a month had now
elapsed since the great Retreat had been brought
to an end by the unaided effort of Italian troops.
The situation now seemed well in hand, and a further
break not at all likely.

There had been a striking scene in the Italian
Chamber about this time, when the Prime Minister,
Orlando, announced that high military opinion had
been opposed to the holding of the Piave line, recom-
mending a further retreat to the line of the Mincio,
or the Adige, or even the Po, which would have
involved the surrender of Venice, Padua, Vicenza
and Verona.   But the Cabinet at Rome had rejected

these recommendations and ordered that the Piave line should be held at all costs, and the valour of the Italian common soldier had triumphed over the forebodings of the generals.

On the 8th, our re-equipment being at last complete, we were warned to join the XIth British Corps on the arrival of our transport. The end of our stay at Ferrara was now in sight, and our last days were full of partings. The Major told me how one morning a little old man, apparently an artisan, ran after him down the road and, speaking excellent French, said how fine the British soldiers looked, and how splendid the news of the capture of Jerusalem was, and then insisted on his going into a café and drinking a glass of vermouth with him and, on parting, held his hand for several moments, gazing into his eyes with a look of affection and pride.

On the 9th a little ceremony took place in the Artillery Mess, where the British officers presented a silver cup, suitably inscribed, to their brother officers of the Italian Artillery. There was a large gathering. My own Major, who was in command of British troops at Ferrara, made the presentation, and the Italian Commandant made an eloquent reply.

On the 10th I told the page boy at the Circolo that the future of the world was in the hands of himself and the rest of the young, and that they must see to it that there were no more wars. This speech made him open his big brown eyes a bit wider ! I had often talked to this boy before, and he was, I think, rather interested in me, thinking me no doubt a queer and unusual sort of person. He used to steal moments to come and enter into conversation with me when none of the older club servants were in sight. If any of them appeared in the distance, he used to pretend that I had called him for the purpose of ordering a drink, and bolt to the bar.

On the 11th another presentation ceremony took place, this time at the Circolo. Those of us who had enjoyed honorary membership here presented to the Club two small silver clocks. The Major again made a short speech and the President of the Club replied, expressing the hope that the hours might be short, which these clocks would record before the hour of final victory. The cordiality of all the members of the Club at this meeting was very memorable. One old gentleman of 76 years of age told me that I was the very image of his son who was serving at the front in the Artillery, and with tears in his eyes kissed me on both cheeks. "Permit this sign of affection," he said, "seeing that here we are in the midst of friends."

That afternoon a few of us had tea for the last time at Finzi's, a favourite haunt of mine between the Castello and the Cathedral. After I had said a few words of farewell, Signor Finzi said to me, in one of those perfectly turned compliments which Italians always pay to foreigners endeavouring to speak their language, "Lei parla la lingua di Dante,"[1] and Signora Finzi gave to each of us a small Italian flag.

That night our transport arrived, and our departure was fixed for the following morning. The 12th of December was a day that I shall vividly remember for the rest of my life. We left Ferrara about 1 p.m.

[1] "You speak the language of Dante."

after one of the most enthusiastic demonstrations I have ever seen. That morning the town had been placarded far and wide with the following poster :—

Comitato di Preparazione Civile.[1]

CITTADINI,
     Stamane alle ore undici e trenta (11.30) gli Artiglieri inglesi muoveranno dal Quartiere Palestro diretti alla Stazione Ferroviaria. Essi partono verso il fronte, per difendere cogli eroici soldati d'Italia e di Francia il conteso e sacro suolo della patria, per combattere la barbaria tedesca, che tenta invano di avanzare contro il baluardo offerto dai petti dei soldati di tre nazioni.

CITTADINI,
     Vi invitiamo ad accorrere ed a portare il vostro saluto ai fedeli e valorosi Alleati. Essi debbono sentire che i vostri cuori palpitano, con loro, di speranza e di fede.
                    FERRARA. 11-12 dicembre 1917,
                         IL PRESIDENTE AVOGLI.

---

[1] *Committee of Civilian Preparation.*
FELLOW CITIZENS,
     This morning at 11.30 a.m. the British Gunners will march out from the Palestro Barracks to the Railway Station. They are leaving for the Front, to defend alongside of the heroic soldiers of Italy and France the disputed and sacred soil of our country, and to combat the German barbarians, who strive in vain to advance against the rampart which is formed by the breasts of the soldiers of three nations.

FELLOW CITIZENS,
     We invite you to be present and to salute our brave and faithful Allies. They should be made to feel that your hearts, in unison with theirs, throb with hope and faith.

By eleven o'clock a large crowd was already gathering outside the Barracks. At half-past we marched
out into the street. In front of us went the municipal
brass band, gay with cocks' feathers, and school-
children carrying four banners on long flagstaffs.
There was tumultuous cheering and clapping from a
dense crowd. Flowers were showered upon us, and
a very handsome girl gave me a bouquet of red roses.
The band played impossible march music, so that we
weren't able to keep much of a step.

But the enthusiasm was intense. Spectators
thronged all the windows overlooking our route,
and the cheering crowd stretched thick and unbroken
along both sides of the street all the way. I noticed
a specially enthusiastic group on the steps of the
Castello, and several busy photographers. In between
the efforts of the band our men sang. Outside the
station we marched past the Italian General Commanding the District. Then we were halted and the
General made a speech. I happened to look round,
and found standing beside me, looking up at me,
wide-eyed and wondering, the page boy from the
Circolo, whom I had harangued on the destiny of the
world's youth, and afterwards tipped. The band
was playing over and over again, at short intervals,
God Save the King, the Marcia Reale, the Marseillaise,
the Brabançonne and the Marcia degli Alpini. Whenever any of these national anthems was played, all
the troops stood at attention, and we officers at the
salute.

Then a little man with a black beard and an eager
manner stepped forward and mounted a chair, and
on behalf of the Association of Italian Teachers wished

us good luck. He spoke in English. He told us that his wife was " an Englishman," and recalled the names of Garibaldi and Gladstone, Palmerston and Cavour. He then presented to the Major an Italian Flag, which was handed to our Battery Sergeant-Major to be carried at the head of the troops as they marched into the station. Many Italian officers were present to say personal good-byes, and an immense crowd was on the platform cheering and singing, and distributing gifts and refreshments to our men. One gift was a little piece of tricolour ribbon, which an old woman gave to one of us. It had a note pinned to it addressed " to a brave British soldier," saying that she had a son at the Front who always carried just such a little piece of ribbon as a talisman, cut off the same roll, and that it had always kept him safe, and that it would keep the British soldier safe too. The note was signed " Tua Madrina " (" your god-mother ").

At last it seemed that everyone was aboard, and the train started. But it was then discovered that the Major, Jeune and Manzoni had been left behind, not expecting the train to start so soon. They had chased it for a hundred yards down the line, but failed to catch it up. So the stationmaster telephoned to Rovigo to stop the train there till the three missing ones arrived, which they ultimately did, riding on an engine specially placed at their disposal. So ended our stay at Ferrara, in a blaze of wild enthusiasm. And I believe that, collectively, we left a very good impression behind us.

11

PART V

A YEAR OF RESISTANCE AND OF PREPARATION

CHAPTER XXVII

IN STRATEGIC RESERVE

OUR train reached Cittadella shortly after dusk. We interviewed a British R.T.O., who had only taken up his duties five minutes' before our arrival, and so not unnaturally knew nothing about us. The Major proposed that the train should be put into a siding and that we should spend the night in it. This was done. We went into Cittadella, but found everything in complete darkness, most of the houses sandbagged, and all shops, cafés and inns closed at dusk by order of the military. We succeeded, however, in getting a meal of sorts, and then went back to the train and turned in early. We were woken up a little after midnight by two British Staff officers, who were very vague and ignorant, but told us to go next morning to San Martino di Lupari, a little village midway between Cittadella and Castel-franco. This we did and found pretty good billets. Monte Grappa loomed over us to the north, deep in snow. I did not go into Cittadella by daylight, but only saw its battlemented outer walls.

VAL BRENTA, THE ASIAGO PLATEAU AND PART OF THE VENETIAN PLAIN

Then for a few days nothing happened, except that everyone seemed to have caught a cold. We were now part of the XIth British Corps, who were concentrated in the surrounding district and formed for the moment a strategic reserve, which might be sent anywhere according to the development of the situation. If nothing particular happened, we should probably go into the line south of the XIVth British Corps on the Piave. If, on the other hand, the Italians were driven back in the mountains to the north of us, or were forced to retire down the Brenta Valley,—and this danger had not yet quite passed, —we should move up the mountains and take over part of the Italian line, with the French probably on our right. We received tracings of several possible lines of defence, on the plain itself and on the near side of the mountain crest, described as the "Blue Line," the "Green Line," etc., which we were required to reconnoitre with a view to finding Battery positions and O.P.'s. They were all very awkward lines to defend, as the enemy would have splendid observation and we practically none at all.

On the 15th the Major went out in the car reconnoitring to the east. He met some Alpini on the road to whom he said, " Fa bel tempo," [1] and they replied, " Le montagne sono sempre belle; " [2] also, an old man who had never seen British soldiers before, and was tremendously excited and pleased, and shouted with joy.

On the 16th the Major went out again with Jeune

[1] " It's beautiful weather."
[2] " The mountains are always beautiful."

and myself to look for Battery positions for the defence
of the line at the foot of the mountains. We went
through Cittadella and Bassano, then southwards
along the Brenta to Nove, and then back through
Marostica and Bassano. Bassano is a delightful old
town, with many frescoes remaining on the outer walls
of the houses, and a beautiful covered-in wooden
bridge over the Brenta.

Marostica charmed me even more. Its battlemented walls are like those of Cittadella and
Castelfranco, but in a better state of preservation
and more picturesque, running up a rocky foothill
behind the town and coming down again,—a most
curious effect. These Alpine foothills for shape and
vegetation are very like the Ligurian hills north of
Genoa and round Arquata.

At San Trinità, just outside Bassano on the road
to Marostica, is a very fine cypress avenue. There
was a possible Battery position here. I noticed also
a row of cypresses standing at intervals of about
fifty yards along a hillside, dark and tall amid
a mass of grass and rocks and brown fallen leaves.
The weather was clear and cold, but the snow
had shrunk to subnormal on the foothills. The
Weather God was still favouring the enemy. It
was very still, though occasionally shells burst over
the Grappa. But the hills muffle the sounds beyond
them.

On the way back we passed a Battalion of Alpini
marching up, many of them very young. I thought
of the Duke of Aosta's latest message to the undefeated Third Army : " A voi veterani del Carso, ed
a voi, giovani soldati, fioritura della perenne prima-

vera italica." [1] Splendid Alpini! They are never false to their regimental motto, " di quì non si passa ! " [2] They never fail. But nearly all the first Alpini, who went forth to battle in May 1915, are dead now.

On the 20th I went out in a side-car with Winterton to look for positions in the hills above Marostica. Reconnaissances of the back lines were now to be discontinued, a sign, we hoped, of diminishing apprehension and an improving military situation. At San Trinità on the way back we collided with an Italian wagon and had to stop for repairs. A number of Italians gathered round, one of whom I discovered to be a priest, conscribed to serve with the Medical Corps. I bantered this man in a friendly way about secret drinking and the confessional and women and paradise, causing uproarious delight among the bystanders. And the priest took it all in excellent part.

On the 22nd we heard that, irrespective of the movements of the rest of the Corps, a special Group of Heavy Artillery was to be formed, including ourselves, to be lent to the Italian Fourth Army in the mountains. There began to be rumours of an offensive on our part.

On the 23rd we made a reconnaissance up the mountains to look for positions. We started through Bassano, which the Austrians had begun to shell the day before with long range guns, starting a trickling, pitiful exodus of terrified civilians. Just before reaching Marostica we struck up a valley running

---

[1] " To you, veterans of the Carso, and to you, young soldiers, flower of the eternal Italian spring."

[2] " No one passes here ! "

northwards past Vallonara. The road soon began
to rise more steeply. It was a war road, broad and
of splendid surface, one of those many achievements
of the Italian Engineers, which entitles them to rank
easily first among the engineers of the great European
Armies.[1] Before the war this road had been in parts
a mere mule track, in parts non-existent. We went
through a number of little Alpine villages, Crosara,
Tortima, Fontanelli, Rubbio. We had soon risen
more than three thousand feet above the plain, which
lay far beneath, spread out gloriously like a richly
coloured carpet, green, white and brown, through
which ran two broad, twisting, silver threads, the
rivers Brenta and Astico. There had been more than
a hundred bends in the road up to this point, but the
gradient was never uncomfortably steep. Snow lay
thick on the higher levels and the pine and fir trees
were all snow-crowned. Sometimes the road ran along
the edge of rocky gorges, dropping sheer for hundreds
of feet below, with a great mountain wall on the other
hand rising sheer above us. The air grew perceptibly
colder as we mounted higher.

We turned out of view of the plain over undulating
snow fields and down a long valley and came out on
a small plateau, screened by a gradual ridge from
the eyes of the enemy. Here we provisionally chose

---

[1] I have seen it stated, by an impartial authority, that there
has been no roadmaking in war time to compare with that of the
Italians on the Alpine and the Isonzo Fronts and in Albania, since
the Napoleonic wars. A distinguished British engineer, with great
experience of roadmaking in many countries, has also told me that
in his opinion the Swedes are the best roadmakers in the world,
the Italians a close second, and the rest of the world some way
behind.

a Battery position close to a small solitary house,
known as Casa Girardi, on the edge of a pine wood.
All round Italian guns were firing in the snow. We
went on to Col. d'Astiago, which would be our probable
O.P. The summit commanded a wonderful view of
the high mountains to the northward, Longara and
Fior, Columbara and Meletta di Gallio, and the sheer
rock face of the Brenta gorge, and the stream far
below, and the great mass of the Grappa rising beyond.

As we came down, lorry loads of Italian troops
passed us going up, Alpini, Bersaglieri, Arditi and
men of the 152nd Infantry Regiment. They cheered
us wildly as they passed, waving their caps and crying,
" Avanti ! Avanti·! Viva l'Inghilterra ! Viva gli
Alleati ! " And as the string of lorries turned round
and round the spiral curves of the road, now high above
us, they were cheering and waving still, until they
disappeared from view.

.   .   .   .   .   .

The Battery ate their Christmas dinner at San
Martino, though the air had been thick with talk of
an immediate move. On this, as on other, occasions
the Major made an excellent speech, in the course of
which he said : " You will be going very soon into
a place where, before this war, no one would have
dreamed that Siege Artillery could go. You were
the first British Battery to be in action in Italy, and
you will probably be the first British Battery to be
in action in the Alps. We shall be very uncomfortable,
at any rate for a time, but we shall pull through all
right, as we always have before. It will be an honour
to be proud of, and an experience to remember for
the rest of our lives. And I know that whatever

happens to us in this coming year, you will all behave as splendidly in the future as you have always done in the past."

The enemy was doing a good deal of night bombing at this period. Treviso and Padua were attacked with great persistency, so much so that the British G.H.Q. decided to move from the latter city to some smaller and more peaceful place. We used to hear the bombing planes coming over nearly every night and explosions more or less distant. They bombed Bassano, Cittadella and Castelfranco, the latter especially because the French had their Headquarters there. But luckily they left San Martino alone, thinking it too small to worry about. There seemed to be no anti-aircraft defences anywhere. But our Air Force soon mitigated the nuisance by raiding their aerodromes, and brought down a number of hostile planes in air fighting.

Our Staff again brought themselves into notice at Christmas by altering our official address from " B.E.F. Italy " to " Italian Expeditionary Force." I heard that the distinguished General, who introduced this reform, estimated that it would hasten victory by several months. But the stupid soldiers and their stupid relatives at home, having got into the habit of using the abbreviation " B.E.F.," shortened the new address to " I.E.F.," and the stupid postal people began to send the letters to India ! And then the distinguished General had to issue another order, pointing out that " this abbreviation is unauthorised " and that " this practice must cease."

In the midst of such excitements the New Year began, and the Major was awarded the D.S.O. for work on the Carso. He was as delighted as a child, and I too was very glad. This decoration, even more than most others, has been much too freely dished out during this war among quite undeserving people, who have simply made an art of playing up to their official superiors. The Major, however, had always been something of a thorn in the side of various Headquarters, and seldom hesitated to speak his mind both to, and of, Colonels and Generals and Staff officers generally. For this reason, and also for others, I consider that he deserved a D.S.O. a great deal more than many who received one.

CHAPTER XXVIII

THE FIRST BRITISH BATTERY UP THE MOUNTAINS

THE Major's words were soon to come true, after many of those delays and conflicting orders of which the victims of war time "Staff work" have profuse experience. On the 7th of January we moved up the mountains into the position previously selected near Casa Girardi. We were the first British Battery to go up. Two others and a Brigade Headquarters were to follow, when it had been seen how we got on. When in doubt, try it on the dog !

It began to snow as we came into Marostica, and we had great difficulty with the lorries even on gentle gradients. The roads were frozen hard and in places very slippery. We managed, however, to reach Casa

Girardi before nightfall and found that our advance
party had put up some wooden huts, and cut some
trees for fuel. All that night the snow came down
in clouds, but the next· day, and the next few
following, were very fine. The sun shone all day long
from a cold, cloudless sky úpon a waste of flashing
snow, with here and there trees sticking out of it,
and strange red morning lights in the sky behind it,
and sweeping winds across it, and in the sunset the ·
white hillsides slowly changed to a mauve pink.
It was a scene of wonderful beauty. But the temperature was ten degrees below zero one day at noon, and
the next day twenty-four below zero at 9 a.m. and
nine above zero at noon.

These conditions were disconcerting to good shooting, the lower temperatures not having been contemplated by those who compiled our range table in
England. But we got all four guns satisfactorily
registered by the second day, to the evident pleasure
of the Italian Colonel under whose command we were
temporarily placed. This man had a somewhat
ferocious appearance and a reputation for great
rudeness, both to his superiors and his subordinates
in the military hierarchy. It was said that, but for
this, he would long ago have been a General. To us,
however, he showed his politer side, patting the Major
on the back and repeating several times " buon
sistema, buon sistema ! "

The physical discomfort of those early days was
great, but we were full of buoyancy and health.
Everything froze hard during the night, one's boots,
one's clothing, if damp when taken off, the ink in one's
fountain pen. In the morning water poured into a

CASA GIRARDI, (THE HOUSE AMONG THE TREES,) AND ITALIAN HUTS

SOME OF OUR BATTERY'S HUTS NEAR CASA GIRARDI

basin froze hard in a couple of minutes and the lather
froze on one's face before one had time to shave.
The Major, breaking through one of the most funda-
mental traditions of the British Army, announced that
no one need shave more than once in three days.
The morning after our arrival we had a discouraging
breakfast. No fire could be got to burn and no tea
had been made. There was nothing to eat except
a few very hard ration biscuits and some eggs boiled
hard the night before, and now frozen through and
through. One cracked the shell and found icicles
beneath, and miserably held fragments of egg in one's
mouth until they thawed!

But gradually, by patient work and organisation,
these early troubles were surmounted. The whole
Battery had been provided with Italian greatcoats
and other Italian mountain equipment,—white Alpine
boots lined with fur, alpenstocks, spiked snow grips,
which could be fastened on to one's boots like skates,
and white clothing to put on over the top of everything
else, to render us invisible against a snowy background.
I used to hear some amusing comments in the Battery
on our Alpine situation. " This is the sort of thing
you see pictures of in books, but . . . ! " " I suppose
folks would pay quids in peace time to see this ! "
" Why, it's like a blooming Cook's tour ! "

Being the first of the British who had been seen in
these parts, we were objects of great interest to the
Italians, who used to collect in crowds to watch our
guns firing. We became great friends with the
members of a mixed Mess not far away, consisting
of two Anti-aircraft Batteries and the personnel in
charge of a large ammunition dump. Between this

Mess and our own there were frequent exchanges of hospitality.

One day an Italian General's car skidded into a ditch close to our position. We supplied a party of men to get it out again and the General, thanking us, asked if there was anything we wanted. The Major told him that we should like two or three more huts and two good stoves for cooking. A few days later these were delivered by the Italian authorities. Our own Brigade Commander, who had now followed us up the mountains with his two other Batteries, noticed these things and asked how we had come by them. When we told him, he seemed displeased, and next day we got an official letter to inform us that " it has come to notice that British units have in some cases recently been approaching the Italian authorities direct. . . . This practice is irregular and must cease. . . . Indents must be submitted through the proper channels." We smiled and obeyed. But we kept our huts and stoves which were better than any which we should have been likely to get " through the proper channels."

We were very short of water except snow water, there being only one waterpoint for all troops within several miles. Here there was a long queue waiting most of the day. It is probably not generally known that it takes ten dixies full of snow, when melted down, to make one dixie full of water. For this and for hygienic reasons snow water was not much use to us. We were not at this time required to fire very much, but we were warned to get acquainted with the surrounding country, as an action of some importance might be coming off before long. This provided the occasion for several reconnaissances.

On January 15th the Major and I went up Monte Costalunga, a few miles to the west. It was a ziz-zag, scrambling track, and it was thawing enough to make everything rather unpleasant. But we gained some useful new knowledge.

On the 24th, Jeune, together with an Italian officer, a telephonist and myself made a long day of it. Starting early, we were on the top of Costalunga about 9 o'clock, were given a guide by an Italian Field Battery on the summit and went on, along a mountain road commanding a magnificent view, to Cima Echar. Here was a good O.P. from which I got my first sight of Monte Sisemol and Asiago, of which part of the *campanile* was at that time still standing. But it was brought down by Italian shell fire very soon afterwards. I remember thinking that the whole Asiago Plateau should be easy to retake, if we only brought up enough guns. Later on I began to realise that it would not be as easy as it looked.

It was impossible to get telephonic communication with the Battery from Cima Echar, so we could not, as we had hoped, do from there some registrations on wire and trench junctions on Sisemol, which were among our allotted targets. We therefore went back to Costalunga, where the Italian Field and Mountain Batteries along the crest were firing away with great vigour, and after an excellent lunch, which had been hospitably prepared for us, went down again into the valley and walked several miles further west to Monte Tondo.

I noticed at lunch, as on several other occasions

lately, a change in the Italian attitude to good weather. They no longer hoped that it would break and so prevent further Austrian offensives. They hoped it would continue and so permit offensives of their own. Their morale was rapidly rising. We had, indeed, received the previous day the artillery portion of an elaborate offensive plan, but no date had yet been fixed for it.

We climbed up Monte Tondo and down the other side and made our way to an O.P. in a front line trench. For fifty yards of the way there was a break in the trench line and we had to run across the open through knee-deep snow. But the Austrians didn't fire. From this O.P. we had again a fine view of Asiago and the country round it. After delays connected with the telephone, we succeeded in registering two targets. While we were firing, all the woods and houses grew rosy in the sunset. It was dark when we finished. We went back with a Major of the Pisa Brigade, a quiet, spare little man, of great energy and exhausting speed of movement. He gave us coffee and showed us maps at his Brigade Headquarters and then sent us on to the Regimental Headquarters, further down the hill, where they gave us rum punch, believing, as all Italians do, that an Englishman is never happy unless he is drinking alcohol. We got back to the Battery in the moonlight.

On January 27th the long expected action began, and our Brigade lost one of its best officers, who was hit in the head in the front line O.P. on Monte Tondo. His steel helmet and the skill of Italian doctors just saved his life, but he was permanently out of the war. The Italians put their best doctors right forward in the advanced dressing stations. All that day we bombarded enemy Batteries and cross roads and barbed wire. Next morning the Italian Infantry carried Col Valbella and Col d'Echele by assault. The day after they took also Col del Rosso, and beat back very heavy counter-attacks. The Sassari Brigade and a Brigade of Bersaglieri specially distinguished themselves. It was an important and useful success. It considerably improved our line between the Asiago Plateau and Val Brenta, it deprived the enemy of the secure use of the Val Frenzela, and it was the first offensive operation of any importance undertaken by the Italians since the great retreat. Its success went to prove that the Italian Army had been effectively reorganised, and that its morale was again high.

From my sleeping hut and from the Battery Command Post I used to hear for days afterwards the Italian Infantry singing in great choruses, far into the night. There was triumph in their songs, and there was ribaldry and there was longing. I thought I knew what dreams were in their hearts, and, if I was right, those dreams were also mine.

The advance left us a long way behind the new front line, and we expected to move our guns forward ; indeed we selected and asked to be allowed to occupy a very good position behind Montagna Nuova. But this was not allowed, and we stayed where we were for another six weeks. It snowed a great deal and we fired very little. But we had plenty to do to keep pathways dug between the guns and the huts ; often we had to clear these afresh every hour.

During this time I made the acquaintance of several

interesting Italians and Frenchmen. Among these
was Colonel Bucci, who had been attached the year
before to the Staff of one of the British Armies in
France. He was now in command of a Regiment of
Field Artillery, including a group of Batteries known
as the Garibaldian Batteries, which were always placed
at their own request in the most forward positions.
I heard that, when he took over this command, he
sent for all his officers and said, " Now here we are,
some old men and some young men and two or three
boys, and we are all here for the same purpose and
I hope we shall all be always the best of good friends.
But, as a matter of convenience, someone has got
to be in command of the others, and I have been
chosen because I am the oldest."

He used to tell an amusing story of an encounter
he had in France with a British officer from one of the
Dominions, who walked into his bedroom late one
night, after a liberal consumption of liquor, and said
he " wanted the fire " and asked if Bucci was " that
Portuguese." Bucci, having persuasively but vainly
asked him to go away, got out of bed and genially
taking him by the shoulders,—he is a powerful man,—
ran him out into the passage. Whereat the British
officer, surprised and protesting, said, " You have
no business to treat me like that. Don't you see
that I am a Major and have three decorations ? "
pointing to his left breast. " Yes," said Bucci, " and
I am a Colonel, and I have some decorations too,
but I don't wear them on my nighty, and I want to
go to sleep."

He had been in Gorizia before Caporetto, and had
kept, as a melancholy souvenir, the maps showing

the line of his own Regiment's retreat. " I call it
the Via Crucis," he said. " I want to go back. I
want to see an advance across the Piave with Cavalry
and Field Artillery. I want to advance at the gallop.
I have applied to be sent down there." He was a
natural leader of men, and I felt that I would willingly
follow him anywhere.

We saw a good deal too of the officers of a French
Observation Balloon. One of their officers was a
tall man, promoted from the ranks, with big upturned
moustaches, a delightful smile and twinkling eyes.
He smoked more cigars than any man I have ever
met. He smoked them, like some men smoke cigarettes,
one after another all the evening, with no interval
between. He came from Marseilles. Another was
from Auvergne, always most elegantly dressed. He
never smoked at all, for he was very proud of his
white teeth. He spoke Italian and German, but no
English. A third was a little blonde Alsatian business
man. He was usually rather quiet, but one evening
I saw him roused, when someone had said something
that displeased him about Alsace. Then he showed
us that he could be eloquent when he chose.

They are very implacable, these Frenchmen. Undoubtedly Clemenceau spoke in their name, when he
said, " my war aim is victory." Another Frenchman
said to me once, " when Clemenceau is speaking, no
one dares to interrupt, for they know it is the voice
of the soldier at the Front speaking." And one can
scarcely wonder that they are implacable. In Alsace-
Lorraine and in the occupied territories of Northern
France, they say that it is known with complete
certainty that the daughters and wives and widows

of many French officers and men have been compelled
to take up their abode in brothels, and there to await
at all hours of the day and night the visits of their
country's enemies. Is it surprising that certain
French Regiments, knowing these things, never take
prisoners ? And can one fail to admire, even if one
does not unconditionally agree with, the soldier who
would fight on and on, until everyone has been killed,
rather than accept anything less than a complete
victory ?

It is all but impossible for a foreigner to measure
the spiritual effects upon a proudly and self-consciously civilised Frenchman of these unpardonable,
brain-rending, heart-stabbing provocations. But the
statesman at home who, drawing good pay and living
in comfort far behind the Front, is ever ready to
declare that his country " shall continue to bleed in
her glory " is a less admirable spectacle. It is his
business to conceive some subtler and more compre-
hensive war aim than bare military victory, and to
make sure that, when he has died safely in his bed
and been forgotten, other men shall not have to do
over again the work which he complacently bungled.
A fighting soldier, who risks his life daily, may speak
brave words, which are indecent on the lips of an
imboscato, whether military or civilian.

CHAPTER XXIX

THE ASIAGO PLATEAU

ABOUT the middle of March the British Divisions moved up from the Montello to the Asiago Plateau, and all the British Heavy Artillery was concentrated in the Asiago sector. We, therefore, moved six miles to the west and found ourselves in support of British, and no longer of Italian, Infantry. Our Brigade ceased to be a " trench-punching " and became a " counter-battery " Brigade. Most of our work in future was to be in close co-operation with our own Air Force.

My Battery was destined to remain here, with two short interludes, for seven months. It was in many ways a very interesting sector. The British held the line between the Italians on their left and the French on their right. To the right of the French were more Italians. The move had amusing features. One compared the demeanour of the lorry drivers of different nationalities. The scared faces of some of the British the first time they had to come up the hundred odd corkscrew turns on the mountain roads, taking sidelong glances at bird's eye views of distant towns and rivers on the plain below, were rather comical. Even the self-consciously efficient and out-wardly imperturbable French stuck like limpets to the centre of the road, and would not give an inch to Staff cars, hooting their guts out behind them. The Italian drivers, on the other hand, accustomed to the mountains, dashed round sharp corners at

full speed, avoiding innumerable collisions by a
fraction of an inch, terrifying and infuriating their
more cautious Allies.   But I only once saw a serious
collision here in the course of many months.

The Asiago Plateau is some eight miles long from
west to east, with an average breadth of two to three
miles from north to south.   On it lie a number of
villages and small towns, of which the largest is Asiago
itself, which lies at the eastern end of the Plateau
and before the war had a population of about 8000.
Asiago was the terminus of a light railway, running
down the mountains to Schio.   The chief occupation
of the inhabitants of the Plateau had been wood-
cutting and pasture.   In Asiago were several sawmills and a military barracks.   Army manœuvres
used often to take place in this area, which gave
special opportunities for the combined practice of
mountain fighting and operations on the flat.   It
was moreover within seven miles of the old Austrian
frontier.   Asiago was hardly known before the war
to foreign tourists, but many Italians used to visit it,
especially for winter sports.

Across the Plateau from north to south ran the
Val d'Assa, which near the southern edge, having
become only a narrow gulley, turned away westwards,
the Assa stream flowing finally into the river Astico.
The Ghelpac stream, which flowed through the town
of Asiago, joined the Assa at its western turn.   Apart
from these two streams the Plateau was not well
watered.   In summer, when the snows had melted,
water was even scarcer on the surrounding mountains.
All our drinking water had to be pumped up through
pipes from the plain.

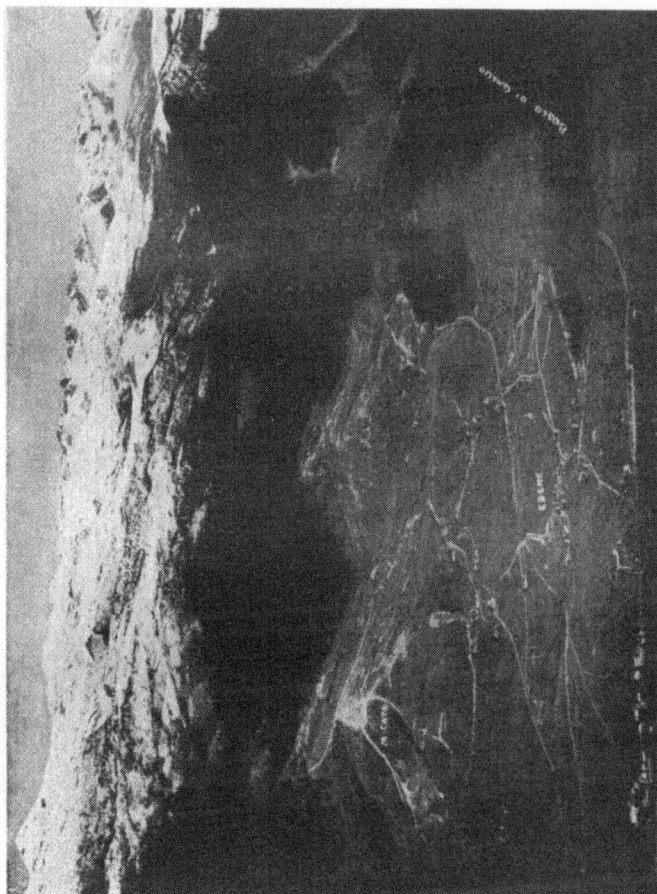

THE EASTERN PORTION OF THE ASIAGO PLATEAU, LOOKING NORTHWARDS. (FROM A BALLOON PHOTOGRAPH)

The Plateau was bounded at its eastern end by
Monte Sisemol, which stands at the head of the Val
Frenzela, which, in turn, runs eastward into the Val
Brenta near the little town of Valstagna. Sisemol
was of no great height and was not precipitous. It
had a rounded brown top, when the snow uncovered
it. But it was a maze of wire and trenches, and a
very strong point militarily. There had been very
bitter fighting for its possession last November and
it had remained in Austrian hands.

At the western end the Plateau was bounded by
the descent to the Val d'Astico. On the northern
side of the Plateau rose a formidable mountain range,
the chief heights of which, from west to east, were
Monte Campolungo, Monte Erio, Monte Mosciagh
and Monte Longara. This range was thickly wooded
with pines, among which our guns did great damage.
I always more regretted the destruction of trees than
of uninhabited houses, for the latter can be the more
quickly replaced. This range was pierced by only
four valleys, through each of which ran roads vital
to the Austrian system of communications, the Val
Campomulo, the Val di Nos, the Val d'Assa and the
Val di Martello. The Austrians had also a few roads
over the top of the mountains, but these were less
good and less convenient.

Along the southern side of the Plateau ran another
ridge, less mountainous than the ridge to the north,
and completely in our possession. This ridge also
was thickly wooded, and pierced by only a few valleys
and roads. The road we came to know best was the
continuation of the wonderful road up from the plain,
through Granezza to the cross-roads at Pria dell' Acqua,

and on through the Baerenthal Valley to San Sisto. Thence it led through the front line trenches into the town of Asiago itself. At Pria dell' Acqua, a most misleading name, where there was no water, but only a collection of wooden huts, another road branched off westwards, running parallel to the front line, behind the southern ridge of the Plateau.

The Italian Engineers had created a magnificent network of roads in this sector of the Front. Before the war there had been only one road into Asiago from the plain. Now there were half a dozen, all broad and with a fine surface, capable of taking any traffic. And, in addition, there were many transverse roads, equally good, joining up and cutting across the main routes at convenient points.

When the British troops took over this sector in March, the whole Plateau, properly so called, was in Austrian hands. It had been taken last November in the mountain offensive which followed Caporetto. At one perilous moment the Austrians had held San Sisto and their patrols had passed Pria dell' Acqua, but they had been thrown back by Italian counter-attacks to the line they now held. Our front line ran along the southern edge of the Plateau, and, on the right, along the lower slopes of the southern ridge, just inside the pine woods. On the left, further west, it ran mostly on the flat and more in the open. Where the Val d'Assa turned west, our front line ran on one side of the shallow gulley and the Austrian on the other. The Austrian front line was completely in the open. The first houses of Asiago were only a few hundred yards behind it.

From the defensive point of view our line was very

strong, and the trenches, particularly at the eastern end, very good, deeply blasted in the rock. The wooded ridge, running close behind our front line all the way, completely hid from the enemy all movement in our rear. He could get no observation here except by aircraft. Even movements in our front line, owing to the trees, were largely invisible at a distance, and, owing to the lie of the ground, large parts of No Man's Land could be seen from our own trenches, but from nowhere in the enemy's lines, with the result that we were able to post machine guns, trench mortars and even, for a short time, a field battery there, without being detected, until these weapons had served their immediate purpose. Our systems of transport, supply and reliefs of the troops in the line could, therefore, be carried out at any hour of the day or night with almost complete disregard of the enemy. His intermittent shelling of the roads was perfectly blind and haphazard and seldom did us any damage.

He, on the other hand, was in a very undesirable situation. Not only was his front line all the way in full view from our various ground O.P.'s, but a long stretch of flat country several miles broad behind his front line was equally in view. Only a few small folds in the ground were invisible from all points along our ridge. We could see also most of the nearer slopes of the northern ridge, though here the thick woods and breaks in the hillside gave him greater opportunities for concealment. Taking into account, therefore, ground observation only, we had him at a tremendous disadvantage. He dared not move nor show himself in daylight behind his line, and was compelled to carry out all his supply and troop movements at night, or during fogs that might lift at any moment. One French Battery did no other work except sweep up and down his roads throughout the hours of darkness, and it is obvious that the probable damage done in this way was far greater than anything he could hope to do to us.

Taking into account the possibilities of observation from the air, the balance in our favour became even greater. We had a strong superiority in the air, whenever it was worth our while to enforce it, partly because our airmen were individually superior to the Austrians, and partly because we had more and better machines. Our pilots often flew over the northern ridge, both to observe and to bomb, but the enemy seldom crossed the southern ridge. His anti-aircraft Batteries were, however, at least as good as ours, and, in my opinion, better.

Most of our pre-arranged counter-battery shoots were carried out with aeroplane observation against enemy Batteries situated in the thick woods on the slopes of the northern ridge, the airman flying backwards and forwards over the target and sending us his observations by wireless. But it was often necessary to spend more than half of the four hundred rounds allotted to a normal counter-battery shoot in destroying the trees round the target, before the airman could get a good view of it. Flying, however, was always difficult on the Plateau, especially during the winter, and more difficult for our men than for theirs, since there were no feasible landing-places behind our lines. Our nearest aerodromes were down on the plain, and a big expenditure of petrol was required to get the airman up the mountains and actually over the Plateau, and also to get him down again. The time during which he could keep in the air for observation was, therefore, very limited. Weather conditions on the Plateau, moreover, were often very unfavourable for flying even in the spring and summer. The practical importance of our superiority in the air was thus smaller than might have been expected.

From the defensive point of view, then, our position was pretty strong. But the sector was important and might at any time become critical, and much depended upon its successful defence. For the mountain wall that guarded the Italian plain had been worn very thin in this neighbourhood by the Austrian successes of last year. An Austrian advance of another few miles would bring the enemy over the edge of the mountains, with the plain beneath in full view. Further defence would then become extremely difficult and costly, and the whole situation, as regards relative superiority of positions and observation, now so greatly in our favour, would be more than reversed. We were too near the edge to have any elbow room or freedom of manœuvre. Our present positions were almost the last that we could hope to hold without very grave embarrassment. It would have seemed evident, then, that to obtain more elbow room and security, we should not be content with a defensive policy, but should aim at gaining ground and thickening the mountain wall by means of an early local offensive, even if larger operations were not yet practicable.

But, from the offensive point of view, our position presented great difficulties. To make only a small advance would leave us worse off than now. Merely to go out into the middle of the Plateau, merely to reoccupy the ruins of Asiago, would be futile, except for a very slight and transitory "moral effect." To carry the whole Plateau and establish a line along the lower slopes of the northern ridge would be no better. We should only be taking over the difficulties of the enemy in respect of his exposed positions, while he would escape from these difficulties and obtain an immunity from observation nearly as great as that which we now possessed. No offensive would benefit us which did not give us, at the very least, the whole of the crest of the northern ridge. And to aim at this would be a big and risky undertaking, involving perhaps heavy casualties and large reserves. We had only three British Divisions in Italy at this time, the 7th, 23rd and 48th, two of which were always in the line and one in reserve. The French had now only two Divisions in Italy and the Italians, when the German advance in France became serious, had sent to France more men than there were French and British left in Italy. The large fact remained that, since the military collapse of Russia the previous year, the Austrians had brought practically their whole Army on to the Italian Front and established a large superiority over the Italians, both in numbers and in guns. Considerable Italian reserves had to be kept mobile and ready to meet an Austrian offensive anywhere along the mountain front or on the plain. There was not likely to be much that could be safely spared to back up a Franco-British offensive on the Plateau. None the less, the value of a successful offensive here was recognised to be so great, that it

was several times on the point of being attempted
in the months that followed. But it did not finally
come, until events elsewhere had prepared the way and
sapped the enemy's power of resistance,

This, however, is anticipating history. In March,
when we first arrived, we moved into a Battery position
in the pine woods behind the rear slope of the southern
ridge. Our right hand gun was only a hundred yards
from the cross-roads at Pria dell' Acqua, disagreeably
close, as we afterwards discovered. For the enemy
had those cross-roads " absolutely taped," as the
expression went. In other respects the Battery
position was a good one. Being an old Italian position,
it had gun pits already blasted in the rock, though
they were not quite suited to our guns and line of fire,
and we had to do some more blasting for ourselves.
In the course of this, a premature explosion occurred,
wounding one of our gunners so severely that he lost
one leg and the sight of both his eyes and a few days
later, perhaps fortunately, died of other injuries.
He was a Cornishman, very young and very popular
with every one in the Battery. We missed him
greatly. In this same accident Winterton was also
injured, and nearly lost an eye. He went to Hospital
and thence to England, and saw no more of the war,
for the sight of his eye came back to him but slowly.

The Italians had also blasted some good *caverne*
in the position, and these we gradually enlarged and
multiplied, till we had cover for the whole Battery.
Being on the side of a hill, and our guns not constructed
to fire at a greater elevation than forty-five degrees
(the Italians had fired at " super-elevations " up
to eighty), we had to cut down many trees in front

of the guns. But this clearance hardly showed in aeroplane photographs, as there were already many bare patches in the woods. We had perfect flash-cover behind the ridge and were, indeed, quite invisible, when the guns were camouflaged, even to an aeroplane flying low and immediately overhead. From our position we could shoot, if necessary, right over the top of the northern ridge, on the other side of the Plateau. And this was good enough for most purposes.

We prepared another position, which was known as the " Forward " or " Battle Position," at San Sisto, about four hundred yards behind the front line. This position we never occupied, but we should have done so, if an offensive had come from our side while we were still on the Plateau. San Sisto, I was told, was once the centre of a leper reservation. There is a little chapel there, but no other buildings. This chapel was used by the R.A.M.C. as a First Aid Post. One day I saw a shell go clean through the roof of it, but there was no one inside at the time.

The Battery O.P. was a glorious place, up a tall pine tree on the summit of Cima del Taglio, a high point to the east of the Granezza—Pria dell' Acqua road. This O.P. had been built by the French. It was reached by a strong pinewood ladder, with a small platform half way up as a resting-place. The O.P. itself consisted of a wooden platform, nailed to cross pieces, supported on two trees. It was about fifteen feet long and four feet broad and some ninety feet above the ground. At one end of the platform a hut had been erected, with a long glass window, opening outward, on the northern side, and a small fixed glass window on the western. The other end of the platform

ROAD BEHIND OUR BATTERY POSITION LEADING TO PRIA DELL' ACQUA.
OUR GUNS WERE ON THE LEFT OF THE ROAD, AND THE FRONT LINE
FURTHER TO THE LEFT AGAIN, ROUGHLY PARALLEL TO THE ROAD

CHAPEL AT SAN SISTO, USED AS A FIRST AID POST, AND ITALIAN GRAVES IN THE
MIDDLE OF OUR BATTLE POSITION

was uncovered. When the weather was bad one could shelter in the hut and imagine oneself out at sea, as the trees swayed in the wind. The O.P. was well hidden from the enemy by the branches of the trees. The view was superb. Immediately below the thick pine forest sloped gradually downwards, the trees still carrying a heavy weight of snow. Among the trees patches of deep snow were visible, hiding rocky ground. Beyond lay the Plateau, studded with villages and isolated houses, with the ruins of Asiago in the centre of the view, and, to the left of it, the light railway line and its raised embankment, along which the Austrian trenches ran. And beyond, more pinewoods on the northern ridge, and beyond, more mountains, one snowy range behind another, up to the horizon. The visibility was often poor and variable from one minute to another. Great clouds used to sweep low over the Plateau, blotting out everything but the nearest trees, and then sweep past, and Asiago would come into sudden view again, and the sun would shine forth once more upon the little clusters of white houses, some utterly wrecked, some mere shells, others as yet hardly touched by the destruction of war. The prosaic name of this O.P. was " Claud."

There was another O.P. called Ascot, which we used sometimes to man at the beginning. It was on, or rather in, Monte Kaberlaba, just behind the front line, approached through a communication trench and then a long tunnel through the rock, named by our troops, the Severn Tunnel. This tunnel was full of water and many worse things, and it was impossible to clean it out properly. The unfortunate telephonists

off duty had to live and sleep in it.   The O.P. was a
cramped, little, stinking place at the far end of the
tunnel, shared with the Italians, undoubtedly visible
and well known to the enemy, and with practically
no view.   The Major, by his usual skilful diplomacy,
soon arranged that we should man Claud permanently,
but Ascot never.

My only pleasant recollection of Ascot is that once,
about midnight, as we were keeping watch together,
a young Italian gunner from the Romagna sang to me.

> " ' Addio, mia bell', addio ! '
>   Cantava nel partir la gioventù,
>   Mentre gl' imboscati si stavano
>   Divertire, giornale in mano
>   E la sigaretta.
>   Per noi l'assalto
>   Alla baionetta !
>   Come le mosche noi dobbiam morir,
>   Mentre gl' imboscati si stanno a divertir." [1]

He sang me also another longer song, composed by
a friend of his, which is not fit for reproduction.

   .   .   .   .   .

We experienced great variations of weather on the
Plateau.   When we first arrived in March the snow

---

[1] " Good-bye, my darling, good-bye ! "
  Sang the young men as they went away,
  While the imboscati were standing about
  To amuse themselves, with a newspaper in their hand
  And a cigarette.
  For us the bayonet charge !
  Like flies we must die.
  While the imboscati stand about to amuse themselves.

This is one of many front line versions of a patriotic drawing-
room song.   It has an admirable tune.

was in full thaw, and every road a sunlit, rushing
torrent. We climbed about at that time in gum boots.
Later it snowed again heavily and often. Sometimes
for several days running we were enveloped in a thick
mist, and then suddenly it would clear away. Once,
I remember, it cleared at night, and one saw the full
moon rising through the pine trees into an utterly
clear, ice-cold sky, and under one's feet the hard snow
scrunched and glittered in the moonlight.

British, French and Italian Batteries were all mixed
together in this sector. On our left came first another
British Battery, then two French, one in front of the
road and one behind it, then another British, then an
Italian. On our right, slightly more forward, the
Headquarters of an Italian Heavy Artillery Group, in
front of them a British and an Italian Battery, one
on each side of the road leading past Kaberlaba to
the front line. To the right of the Italian Headquarters, across the San Sisto road, was a French
Battery, with two Italian Batteries in front of it.
To our own right rear was one Italian Battery and
two French, and in rear of them, back along the road
to Granezza, our own Brigade Headquarters.

This mixture was a good arrangement, stimulating
friendly rivalry and facilitating *liaison* and exchange
of ideas. Our relations were specially cordial with
the Italian Group Headquarters and with one of
the French Batteries on our left. The Italian Major
commanding this Group was a Mantuan and he and
I became firm friends. It was in his Mess one night,
in reply to the toast of the Allies, that I made my
first after-dinner speech in Italian. I do not claim
that it was grammatically perfect, but all that I said

was, I think, well understood, and I was in no hesitation for words.

Not till the end of May did Spring really climb the mountains, and the snow finally vanish, and then the days, apart from the facts of war, were perfect, blue sky and sunshine all day long among the warm aromatic pines and the freshness of the mountain air. Here and there, in clearings in the forest, were patches of thick, rich grass, making a bright contrast to the dull, dark green of the pines, and in the grass arose many-coloured wild flowers.

The Italians have buried their dead up here in little groups among the trees, and not in great graveyards. There was one such little group on the hillside in the middle of our Battery position, between two of our gunpits. There was another in the middle of our forward position at San Sisto, and another, where some thirty Bersaglieri and Artillerymen were buried, in the Baerenthal Valley. It was here one day that an Irish Major, newly come to Italy, said to me, " I don't want any better grave than that." Nor did I. It was a place of marvellous and eternal beauty, ever changing with the seasons. It made one's heart ache to be in the midst of it. It was hither that they brought in the months that followed many of the British dead, who fell in this sector, and laid them beside the Italians, at whose graves we had looked that day.

CHAPTER XXX

SOME NOTES ON NATIONAL CHARACTERISTICS

FOR a week or two in May an Italian Engineer officer messed with us. He had a sleeping hut on the hill just behind us, and was in charge of a party of men who were working on British Field Artillery positions. His men were on British rations and did not altogether like them. They would have preferred more bread and less meat and jam, and they missed their coffee. Our tea they did not fancy. The first time it was issued to them, they thought it was medicine. " Why do the English give us ' *camomila* ' ? " they asked their officer, " we are not ill ! "

.   .   .   .   .   .

I have had, at one time and another, much gay and delightful intercourse both with Frenchmen and Italians, which has led me to certain speculative comparisons and to many dangerous generalisations, some of which I will venture tentatively to set down here. But it is difficult to find forms of words which are not mere journalism.

Italian humour is more primitive and uproarious than French, and the Italians seem to present fewer barriers to intimacy, but the proportion of rational discussion is larger in the conversation of the French. Both the French and the Italians combine natural and easy good manners with great punctiliousness in small matters of etiquette. Only very arrogant or very boorish people find it difficult to get on well with either.

13

It is idle for any wideawake observer to deny that a certain antipathy exists between the French and the Italians. Both, I think, generally prefer the British to their Latin brothers, and I have heard both say unjust and absurdly untrue things about the other. Their antipathy is rooted partly in temperament, partly in history, and partly in that ignorance and lack of understanding which accounts for nine-tenths of all international antipathies. As Charles Lamb said, in an anecdote which President Wilson is fond of quoting, " I cannot hate a man I know." It is sometimes said that the French and the Italians are too much alike to be in perfect sympathy. The Frenchman has at times an instinct to be what an Englishman would call " theatrical," which instinct the Englishman himself hardly possesses at all. But in the Italian this instinct is even stronger than in the Frenchman, and he gives it freer play. Thus the Frenchman often notices the Italian doing and saying things which he himself dislikes, but which it needs a deliberate effort of self-repression on his part not to imitate. The Englishman has no inclination to do and say such things, and is, therefore, more tolerant of them than the Frenchman, thinking them either charming or merely " queer," according to his temperament.

If the French are the more admirable, the Italians are the more lovable; if the French are the more creative, the Italians are the more receptive. In the French, though not so much in the Italians, one does find that " sheer brutality of the Latin intellect," which, since the French Revolution, has dethroned many previously dominant ideas and institutions.

One finds in the French a tradition of limpid precision, of concise and ordered logic, while the Italians are still groping rather turgidly among those great abstract ideas which the French handle so easily. The spirit of France shines with the hard splendour of the noonday sun, of Italy with the soft radiance of the light of early mornings and late afternoons.

The French are proud and sometimes intolerant, the Italians tolerant and often diffident. It has been truly said that in every modern Frenchman there is still something Napoleonic, however subconscious it may have become. One could never be surprised if, in the midst of conversation, a Frenchman should suddenly draw himself up and cry " Vive la France, monsieur ! " But one does not expect an Italian in like circumstances to cry " Viva l'Italia ! " In general, the French are the more tenacious and clear-visioned in adversity, but none are more irresistible in success, nor more conscious of its drama, than the Italians.

The low birth-rate of France, as compared with Italy, is a fact of deep and permanent importance. In years to come the French will grow more and more negligible, numerically, in world politics, but the French spirit is immortal and unconquerable. It will penetrate the hearts of the best men for ever, and ideas characteristically and originally French will continue to mould the world's thought and action till the end of time. The Italians on the other hand will play in future history a greater part numerically, and moreover, by a greater intermarriage with other races, will continue to produce fine and generous human types, not wholly Italian. Italians will continue to

show a shining example to the world by reason of their
gaiety and charm of character, their mental subtlety,
which with time will grow less involved and more lucid
in expression, by their art of life, even now not much
inferior to the French, by their sensitiveness to beauty,
by their capacity for enthusiastic appreciation, and
by their technical genius in applied science.

Italy is a naturally democratic and peaceable
polity, and her present imperfections will diminish
rapidly with the increase of her national maturity
and stability. She will be a sane and healthy element
in the future international order.

In some respects, as in their indifference, sometimes
excessive, to foreign opinion, the French resemble
the British, just as, in their excessive sensitiveness
on this point, the Italians resemble the Americans.
This is the contrast between age and youth, between
nations with a continuous tradition of centuries behind
them and nations born or reborn only yesterday.

There remains the larger contrast between the
Latins on the one hand and the Anglo-Saxons on the
other. At first sight it is the latter who are the more
realistic and the more practical, the former who are
the more effusive, idealistic and poetical. But, as
Mr Norman Douglas admirably puts it in *South Wind,*
" Enclosed within the soft imagination of the *homo
Mediterraneus* lies a kernel of hard reason. The
Northerner's hardness is on the surface ; his core, his
inner being, is apt to quaver in a state of fluid irre-
sponsibility." The comparative method of approach
to the institution of marriage among Latins and among
Anglo-Saxons illustrates this truth. And it serves
also, perhaps, for an example that, in the midst of the

terrors of war, the dim project of a League of Nations, the only hope of the world, first took shape in the minds of Anglo-Saxon dreamers and not of Latin realists. The Latin often thinks more clearly, but not always more profoundly, than the Anglo-Saxon. The currents on the surface are not always the same as the currents in the deep.

CHAPTER XXXI

ROME IN THE SPRING

I WAS at Rome in May. Of the many things and persons I saw there, not much is relevant here. But there is an intoxication and a beauty and a sense of wonder in Rome in the Spring, as great as I have found at any time elsewhere. Rome grew upon me, rapidly and ceaselessly, during the few days that I spent there, and sent me back to the mountains, clothed with their pinewoods and their graves of much brave youth, uplifted in heart and purified in spirit.

.   .   .   .   .   .

Early one afternoon in the Piazza Venezia I fell in with two Italian officers, an Alpino and an Engineer, both wounded and not yet fit to go back to the Front. We rapidly made friends, and, having drunk beer together, we took a carrozza and drove to the Villa Borghese Gardens, where we walked and sat for several hours. Then we went back to the Piazza Venezia, and walked in the neighbourhood and contemplated the monuments. My friends said that Rome was the capital city of the world, and praised also the giant memorial to Italian Unity and Victor Emmanuel II., which, still unfinished, dominates the Piazza, and indeed a large part of the city. This memorial is, I believe, condemned by the greater part of foreign æsthetic opinion, the Germans alone conspicuously dissenting. Personally I like it in the fading light from close at hand, and in a bright light from a distance, as one sees it, for instance, from the Pincio.

We spoke a little, but not much, of the war. They were both for fighting on till final victory, whatever the cost, and both spoke with admiration of the inflexible and stubborn spirit of the British nation. Very wonderful too is the spirit which animates the Alpini. My Alpino friend had been wounded in the leg last August at Rombon, and still walked lame. He told me of incidents which he had witnessed, of Alpini charging across and through uncut enemy wire, with the wounded and the dying crying to their comrades, " Ciao ! [1] Ciao ! Avanti ! " He sang me also certain songs of the Alpini, in one of which they sing that in the Italian tricolour the green stands for the Alpini,[2] the white for the snow on their mountains and the red for their blood. O these " fiamme verdi," who can talk and sing themselves into such transfigured ecstasies, as to turn death and pain almost into easy glories !

The three of us dined at a little restaurant near the

---

[1] " Ciao " is a colloquialism, much the same as our own " so long," or " good-bye and good luck ! " It is an intimate word, used only between friends at parting.

[2] The regimental colours of the Alpini are plain green, worn on the collar.

Pantheon, and my friends wrote their names and a greeting to my wife on a post card, and an old man at the next table ordered a bottle of wine, in which we all drank the health of the Allies, and a party at another table began to sing, and went on singing for nearly an hour. We stayed in that restaurant talking till eleven p.m., when the lights were turned out, and then my friends demanded that we should make another " giro artistico," which terminated beneath Trajan's Column, where in the warm air we sat and talked for half an hour more, and separated about midnight, I having had eight hours of continuous practice in the use of the second person singular of Italian verbs.

Next day I lunched with my friends the Marinis, at their charming Villa on Monte Parioli, and in the afternoon Signor Marini offered to act as my guide to places of interest. We took the tram to the Piazza del Popolo, which was laid out in 1810 under the French Empire, perfectly circular and symmetrical, thus differing from the more Italian of Roman Piazzas, such as the elongated and quite unsymmetrical Piazza di Spagna. We passed along the broad embankment beside the Tiber and through the Square of St Peter's. Just outside the gates of the Vatican, my guide pointed out to me the little shabby building occupied by the Giordano Bruno Society, symbolic of the brave defiance thrown out, all down the ages, by poverty and the spirit of freedom and intellectual honesty, in the face of wealth and power and oppression, intellectual bondage and the dead weight of tradition.

My guide thought that, out of the wreck of her

material defeat and disaster, Russia would perhaps give a new spiritual religion to the western world, to take the place of old forms now dead, and historic organisations which, having lacked the audacity and the wisdom to remain poor when riches were within easy reach, had now become visibly and irremediably detached from the life of the people. He did not fear, as some did for France, a clerical revival in Italy after the war. For the Italian branch of clerical power had shown itself in the hour of Italy's deadly peril to be largely lacking in Italian patriotism, and to have been scheming for the maintenance, if not the expansion, of Austrian dominion, and, perhaps, for the re-establishment by the aid of Austrian and German bayonets, or Turkish, if it had been necessary to solicit them, of the Temporal Power of the Papacy over Italian citizens and Italian soil. I saw one of the Swiss mercenaries of the Papacy gazing forth a little contemptuously through a door of the Vatican upon the secular outer world.

From St Peter's we drove up the Janiculum, stopping on the way at the convent of S. Onofrio, where Tasso passed the last three weeks of his life and where a Tasso Museum has been accumulated. Very admirable is the equestrian statue of Garibaldi on the Janiculum, both as sculpture and for its details of intention, such as that sideways turning of his head, looking down hill at the Vatican, as though saying, " Non ti dimentico,"—" I do not forget you, my old enemy." The view of Rome from this point is magnificent, the best that I have seen, though the view from the Pincio only just falls short of it.

Thence, passing outside the old city walls through

the Porta San Pancrazio, we stood on ground made memorable by Garibaldi's defence of the Roman Republic in 1849, and went down, past the Pope's monument to the French who died fighting to defend his Temporal Power against the Garibaldini, into the beautiful garden of the Villa Pamfili. "Attendono il finale risorgimento," [1] says the Pope's Italian version on the monument. It is an ironical phrase in view of the history of the next twenty years. "They did not have long to wait," I said, "a bird in the hand is worth two in the bush." And my guide said, I thought well, of the French that they are a people of great gifts and of most generous mind, but that their rulers have often showed "un po' di volubilità, un po' di fantasia."

We visited last of all the Depôt of the Bersaglieri in Trastevere, where is also the famous Bersagliere Museum. Here we were received and shown round with great courtesy by the Colonel commanding the Depôt, a handsome man with most sad eyes, but full of great regimental pride in this creation, intimately and characteristically Italian, of General La Marmora.

In the Museum, among much that was trivial, I found much that was interesting and even deeply moving : the relics of Enrico Toti, an artist who, having only one leg, joined the Bersaglieri Ciclisti as a volunteer at the beginning of the war, and rode up mountain tracks on a bicycle with a single pedal, and died, after acts of the greatest heroism and after sustaining for many hours grave wounds, crying with his last breath "Avanti Savoia !", upon whose

[1] "They await the final resurrection." But "risorgimento" to most Italians suggests modern history more than theology.

dead body and brave departed spirit was conferred
the most rare Gold Medal for Valour ; photographs
of all the Bersaglieri, who since the foundation of the
Regiment have won the Gold Medal, some twenty of
them, hanging together on one wall, all dead now ;
the steel helmet of a Bersagliere Major, killed on the
Carso, while leading his men ; this is all that they
found of him, but it has three holes through the front,
sufficient proof, said the Colonel, that he was not
going backward when he died ; a menu card, signed
by all the officers of a Bersagliere Battalion, who
dined together on the eve of the victorious action of
Col Valbella last January, in which they played a
worthy part.

The Colonel told me that his own son was killed and
is buried beyond the Isonzo, near Cervignano. It
had been suggested to him that he should have the
body brought home, but he preferred to leave it where
it fell. " C'è un' idea che è morta lì," he said, " It
is an idea which has died there. Some day, if I live,
I shall make a pilgrimage thither, but the Austrians
may, by now, have destroyed the grave."

Outside in the courtyard, where the Colonel took
leave of us, I saw many young Bersaglieri, the latest
batches of recruits, mere boys. " They are splendid
material," he said, with a military pride, not without
a half-regretful tenderness, " one can make anything
out of them." They were, indeed, incomparable
human stuff, whether for the purposes of peace or war.
They seemed to have the joy of the spring in their
eyes, just as that middle-aged Regular soldier had
in his the sadness of autumn. And amid all the
beauty of Rome in the spring, I was haunted by the

grim refrain, " Nella primavera si combatte e si muore,
o soldato,"—" In the springtide men fight and die,
young soldier."

.   .   .   .   .   .

I went away from Rome strengthened in my previous
judgment that the Italians are not a militarist nation.
There was no sign of the militarist, as distinct from
the military, spirit at the Bersagliere Depôt. The
relations of the Colonel and Signor Marini illustrated
this. They had never met, nor, I think, heard of one
another before. Yet this little civilian seemed to find it
quite natural to march into a military barracks without
any preliminary inquiries, to walk upstairs and
straight into the Commanding Officer's office and,
not finding the Commanding Officer there, to send a
message into the Officer's Mess, and, the Commanding
Officer having come out, to present his card, without
any appearance of servility or undue deference, and
to ask to be taken round. And the Colonel seemed
to see nothing odd in these proceedings, but placed
himself at once at our disposal and showed us everything and talked without aloofness and without reserve
to both of us. I could not help thinking that things
would not have happened quite like this at the Depôt
of a crack regiment in most other European capitals.

CHAPTER XXXII

THE FIFTEENTH OF JUNE, 1918

I HAPPENED to be the officer on duty in the Battery Command Post on the night of June 14th-15th. There had been a thick fog for several days and not much firing. No one expected anything unusual. The Battery was much below strength owing to the ravages of what the doctors in the mountains called " mountain fever " and the doctors on the plain called influenza. We had, if I remember rightly, about forty men in Hospital owing to this cause alone. I myself had a touch of it, but, thinking I could probably count on a quiet night, I refused the offer of a brother officer to take my place, coldly calculating that a few nights later, when it would be my turn to take his duty, I might have more to do. But my hopes of much sleep were soon dispersed.

Orders came in from Brigade for an elaborate counter-battery shoot with gas shell, in two parts, one between 11 p.m. and midnight, the other between 2 and 3 a.m. We had never fired gas shell from six-inch howitzers before, though we had been warned that we should soon be required to do so. We had no gas shell in the Battery, but we were informed by Brigade that a sufficient quantity would arrive by the time the shoot was to begin. In fact, however, the first consignment of gas shell was not delivered in time to enable us to take part in the first part of the bombardment, and I was told not to fire high explosive instead, as that would tend to disperse the gas which other Batteries would be simultaneously firing on the same targets. The method adopted on this and later occasions, when gas was used, was that a number of our own Batteries should concentrate for, say, five minutes at the fastest rate of fire possible on a particular enemy Battery, then all switch together to another enemy Battery, and so on, all coming back together on to the first enemy Battery after an interval sufficient to lull the human elements forming part of the target into a delusive sense of security and a return to slumber without their masks, or, alternatively, to make them wear their masks continously for prolonged hours of expectation, thus subjecting them to much discomfort, depriving them of sleep, lowering their morale, and making them likelier victims for fresh forms of devilment in the morning. War is a filthy thing, and must be stamped out ruthlessly. The facts of gas will have helped to drive this simple conviction into many a thick, egotistical, unsensitive head. But, as has been wisely said, you cannot half make a war of the modern sort, you cannot let a faint savour of regret hang about all your actions, and enervate your will. And, in plain, brutal truth, our employment of gas was a big factor in determining and hastening the end. Of the military efficiency of our gas tactics we had much evidence later on.

We joined in the second part of the gas bombardment in the early hours of the 15th of June, and, when this was nearly over, I got orders to fire at my leisure ten rounds of high explosive at " Archibald," which was our code name for a certain Austrian searchlight, which used to sweep round the country from the summit of Monte Mosciagh on the far side of the Plateau. So I fired the ten rounds, and the officer at one of the O.P.'s, whom I had previously warned of my intention, reported that Archibald had gone out after the fourth round, and that, judged by the flashes of their explosions, all the rounds had seemed pretty near. It was now nearly half-past three, and, conscious that I had a high and rising temperature, I determined to lie down and get a few hours' sleep. Some of the gas shell which had been intended for the first part of the bombardment, but had arrived about four hours too late, was still being unloaded from lorries on the road outside. But I asked a Corporal to look after this, and send the unloading party to bed as soon as they had finished.

I had just fallen asleep when the Corporal awakened me. Were the men, he asked, to go on unloading the shell ? Still half asleep, I asked why not ? He said that the road was being shelled. I pulled myself together and went to the door of the Command Post. Not only the road, but the whole Battery position and apparently the whole area for some distance round, was being bombarded very violently. So I ordered every one to take cover. It was just 3.45 a.m.

I thought for a moment that this was merely Austrian retaliation for our first use of gas and for the shots at Archibald. In fact, it was the beginning of the big Austrian offensive, which had long been prearranged. During the last few days the Austrians had brought up a large number of new guns to our sector, and had placed a number of them right out in the open. And owing to the thick fog our airmen had been able to see nothing. The bombardment continued with great fury for several hours, with guns of all calibres, but fortunately mostly small, with shrapnel, high explosive, and gas, chiefly lacrimatory, but mixed with a certain quantity of lethal. Luckily we had pretty good cover, mainly *caverne* blasted in the rock. The Command Post itself was proof against anything less than a direct hit from a pretty heavy shell. It was also supposed to be gas proof, but was not. I collected about half a dozen men in it who had nowhere else to go, including two A.S.C. lorry drivers.

Early on, a young Bombardier was hit rather badly in the leg just outside. We brought him into the Command Post, bandaged his wound and laid him on the camp bed, on which I had been hoping to get some sleep, and there left him till the shelling should abate and it should be reasonably safe to carry him to the dressing-station a quarter of a mile away. He lay there, I remember, looking like a little tired cherub, and another Bombardier sat beside him and tried to persuade him to go to sleep. They were very great friends, those two boys, both signallers, and inseparable both on and off duty. The one who was not wounded went out that same morning and spent hours repairing telephone lines under very heavy fire, for which act he won the Military Medal. The other, months later, when his wound was healed and he had returned to the Battery, also won the Military Medal for gallantry on the Piave.

The conduct of the two lorry drivers afforded a strong contrast in psychology. One, a man of middle age, was superbly cheerful. " They can't keep this up much longer," he said several times with a placid smile, " they haven't the stuff to do it." The other, though younger, was a bunch of visible nerves. A shell exploded just behind the Command Post and violently shook the whole structure and a storm of stones hit the log framework. He collapsed on the floor, and was convinced for a couple of minutes that he had been hit, and for some time after that he was suffering from shell shock.

Such illusions come easily at such times. A gas shell made a direct hit on one of our smaller dug-outs. A Sergeant inside was badly gassed. They put him for the moment in a gas-proof shelter, higher up the hill, and several hours later I saw him being carried away on a stretcher, apparently lifeless. But he finally pulled through. A gunner who was with him in the dug-out came running into the Command Post crying out that he also was gassed. I made him lie flat on the floor, and told him to keep as quiet as he could. And then I watched his breathing. It was clear after a minute or two that, if he had had a breath of gas at all, it was only of the slightest. But, when I told him this, he was very unwilling to believe me. Another man was hit just outside, and lay on the ground screaming like an animal in pain. Him, too, we carried into the Command Post, and, later, on a stretcher to the dressing station.

Meanwhile all the telephone lines had gone owing to the shelling, cutting us off from Brigade, other Batteries and O.P.'s. But intermittent communication was maintained by runners, and signallers were out, hour after hour, mending breaks in the line and showing their invariable gallantry. Till about

six o'clock our orders were to lie low, to keep under
cover and not to open fire. The rain of shells continued
without slackening. We were wonderfully lucky to
get off as lightly as we did. It is one of the most
extraordinary phenomena of war, how many shells
can fall in a position of no great size, and yet do very
little damage. It was estimated, and I think quite
soberly, that at least two thousand rounds were
pumped into our Battery position that morning.

It was soon after six that we got orders, passed
along from the next Battery up the road, to open
fire on our " counter-preparation target." This was
a sign that the advance of the Austrian Infantry
had either begun, or was thought to be imminent.
They attacked, in fact, about a quarter to seven
on our sector. Their synchronising was faulty, as
between the different sectors attacked. Some went
forward earlier and others later than had been intended. They were all newly equipped and were
carrying full packs and blankets on their backs.
They had been told by their officers that this was to
be the last great offensive of the war, that they were
going to drive us headlong down the mountain side,
that after two days they would be in Verona, and
after ten days in Rome. They were not told that
they had British troops in front of them. They
came forward bravely and with great determination,
in five successive waves.

On the British left Divisional Front, to the west of
us, they gained a large initial success, and pushed
us back well behind our first line of guns. Here for
some time the situation looked serious. But next
day strong counter-attacks by British and Italian

14

troops restored the line, our lost guns were retaken and the retreating Austrians suffered great slaughter and demoralisation.

On the British right Divisional Front, in support of which our Brigade was operating, the British 23rd Division fought a fight worthy of their high reputation. Forced back for a while from their front line trenches, after a prolonged and intense bombardment and by an overwhelming superiority of numbers, they never even fell back to their support line. But, turning on the enemy who was advancing along and astride the San Sisto road, they drove him back and re-established their own front line within six hours of the first attack. It was here that a boy Colonel, a Sherwood Forester scarcely twenty-one years old, won the V.C. and fell severely wounded. When things looked black, he had organised the defence and the subsequent counter-attack, collecting together British Infantrymen of several Battalions, together with British Artillery-men and Italian Machine-Gunners and Engineers, welding them into a coherent force and making swift, yet well thought out, dispositions which did much to save the situation,.

On the right of the British, the French Infantry, though furiously assaulted, never, I believe, budged an inch. On the right of the French, the Italians were momentarily driven from Col Valbella, Col del Rosso and Col d'Echele, which they had won in January, but retook all three a few days later.

But we in the Battery knew nothing of all this at the time. We knew only that we had to open fire on our counter-preparation target. The gunpit of our No. 1 gun near the cross-roads was in low-lying ground, now so full of gas that one could hardly see one's hand before one's face. Fortunately we could achieve the rate of fire required by using three guns only, so we left No. 1 out of action for the time. The enemy's bombardment, as far as we were concerned, was beginning to slacken a little, but was still heavy. The Major, out on the road with a signaller mending wire, was hit in the face with shrapnel. It turned out, happily, not a serious wound, but at the time it looked less hopeful. He went down the mountains in the same Field Ambulance with the young Colonel of the Sherwood Foresters, of whom I have already spoken.

There was an abandoned Field Ambulance in the road, half in the ditch, with the engine still running. The driver had found the shelling too hot to stay. There was no one inside it, but we got a couple of stretchers from it. And we had need of them. No. 4 gun, my own gun, which was nearest to the road, suffered most severely. Seven of the detachment on this gun were hit, not all at once but, what is apt to be much more demoralising, at intervals of a few minutes. A Bombardier was in charge of the gun that day, no senior N.C.O.'s being available. He showed a very wonderful coolness and courage. Shells were bursting all round the gunpit, and sometimes in the gunpit itself. But the rate of fire never slackened. Every now and again the cry was heard " another casualty on No. 4 ! " and stretcher bearers would start down the road from the Command Post. But, each time, almost before they had started, came the deep report of another round fired. No casualties and no shelling could silence her. At one time this

Bombardier had only two other men to help him work the gun. And both of them were as undismayed as he. He won the Military Medal for his gallantry that day, and I was very proud of him and of No. 4.

The Brigade Chaplain appeared in the course of the morning and gave a hand in carrying the wounded away on stretchers. It was outside his official work and I give him all credit and respect for the help he gave us. But one N.C.O. in the Battery, with the plain speaking that comes naturally in the face of common danger, said to him, " Well, Sir, we never thought much of you before, either as a man or as a preacher, but we're glad to see you here to-day doing your bit."

The Austrian gunners had a fine sense of discrimination in their targets. The wooden hut, in which I and two of my brother officers used to sleep, had been hit two or three times that day, and much of our kit had been destroyed. So had both volumes of Morley's *Rousseau*, which were on a shelf over my bed, leaving behind only a few torn and scattered pages. Much damage had also been done to a collection of Pompeian photographs of great historical interest. But Baedeker's *Northern Italy*, which lay alongside, had not been touched !

.   .   .   .   .   .

The God of Battles also discriminates delicately. He takes the best and leaves the worst behind. There died that day, struck by a shell at the foot of our tree O.P. on Cima del Taglio, one of the finest personalities in the Battery, a signalling Bombardier who had worked for some years on a railway in America and, just before the war, as a railway clerk in the Midlands. He was the father of a young family, thoughtful and capable, and loyal without subservience to those of higher military rank, in so far as he judged them to be worthy of his loyalty. I remember one night at the beginning of the year, when we were keeping watch together among the snows at Col d'Astiago, with the sky cold and clear and full of stars, and when he and I talked in complete understanding and agreement of the waste of war and the deeper purposes of life and the need to build up a better world. Now he is buried in the beautiful Baerenthal Valley, along which runs the road from Pria dell' Acqua to San Sisto and Asiago.

As that day ended, which the Italians always afterwards spoke of as " il giorno quindici " (the fifteenth day), the firing on both sides in our sector slackened, though our guns were seldom silent for more than an hour at a time, and the Austrians still carried out sudden bursts of vicious fire in our neighbourhood. But that night, and the next day and the next, we began to get through information of what had been happening all along the line. And when, a week later, the whole tale could be told, it was evident that no great offensive on any Front during this war, prepared with so great elaboration and carried out with so great resources, had ever quite so blankly failed, as the great Austrian offensive from the Astico to the Sea. And the effect upon the self-confidence and morale of the Italian Army and of the Allied contingents was correspondingly great. For, to speak frankly, this offensive had been awaited with much apprehension and anxiety, with the memory of

Caporetto not yet faded and in view of the success of the German offensive in France.

CHAPTER XXXIII

IN THE TRENTINO

THE Austrian offensive on the mountain sector, from the Astico to Monte Grappa, had been obviously and decisively broken by the 18th of June. But there was still danger on the plain, particularly in the Montello sector, where the Austrians were established in strong force west of the Piave. A flying Brigade of British Heavy Artillery was hurriedly formed and sent down the mountains. Of this Brigade my own Battery formed part. Our general function was to reinforce the Italian Artillery in what was at the moment the most critical sector of the whole Front, our particular function to destroy by shell fire the Piave bridges behind the Austrian troops. But when we arrived we found that the emergency had already passed. The bridges had already been destroyed by airmen and Italian Artillery, and the Austrian forces had either been driven back across or into the river by Italian counter-attacks, or had been cut off and compelled to surrender. We, therefore, came back to the Plateau without firing a round.

But we did not remain there long. The idea of a mobile Artillery of manœuvre was much talked of at this time, and early in July a Brigade consisting of three British Siege Batteries, my own included, was moved westwards up into the Trentino. We travelled all the way by road, through Verona up to Brescia, "the eagle that looks over Lombardy," and thence beside Lake Idro, up the Val Chiese, past Storo into the Val D'Ampola.

All this last stretch of country is famous in Italian history as the scene of Garibaldi's campaign of 1866, which, had it not been interrupted by the course of events elsewhere, would probably have hastened the liberation of Trento by more than half a century, and greatly modified the problems of Italian policy in recent years. The story is well known of the recall of Garibaldi, which reached him at the moment of victory at Bezzecca, and of his famous reply, a model of laconic self-discipline, in the one word " Ubbidisco "—" I obey." The little town of Bezzecca lay this July behind the Italian lines, but in full view and easy range of the Austrians. A company of Arditi was billeted here, with whom I lunched one day, returning from a front line reconnaissance. The Piazza had been renamed by the Italians " Piazza Ubbidisco," and under cover of darkness they set up one night on the mountain side just above the town a memorial stone to Garibaldi and his volunteers of 1866, a provocative target for Austrian gunners.

No other British troops, except these three Batteries of ours, ever fought in the Trentino. It was a proud distinction and a very memorable experience. The natural scenery was superb, a series of great mountain ranges, uneven lines of jagged peaks, enclosing deep cut valleys, the lower slopes of the mountains densely wooded, the higher levels bare precipitous rock. The Austrian front line ran along one ridge of peaks and ours along another ; between ran a deep valley, all No Man's Land, into which patrols used to climb down at night, often with the aid of ropes. One mountain mass, a continuation of Cima d'Oro, was partly in our possession and partly in theirs, and up there by night among the rocks patrols grappled for the mastery, poised high above the world, and in these struggles men sometimes slipped, or were thrown, to crash to death thousands of feet below in the Val di Ledro.

This country was Austrian before the war, though inhabited wholly by Italians, and Italian troops had conquered it with extraordinary feats of endurance and daring in their first great onrush all along their old frontiers in the spring of 1915. But now a big advance here by either side, in the face of carefully prepared opposition, seemed almost inconceivable, except as the result of some wide turning movement, hinging on some point many miles away.

The special military problems presented by warfare in such country were numerous and difficult. Our guns had to be dragged into position up a rough mountain track, which at some points was too narrow and at others too weak to allow the passage of a six-inch howitzer without much preliminary blasting and building up. Our first gun to go up took twenty-four hours of continuous labour between the time of starting up the track and the time of arriving in position, a distance of only about two miles of zig-zag. No tractor or other power engine could be used here. The only force available was that of men hauling on drag ropes, and a party of sixty Italian gunners reinforced our men.

What may be called the problems of pure gunnery were still more difficult. British Heavy guns had never fired under such conditions before and, for the benefit of such of my readers as may be practical Artillerymen, it may be interesting to remark that for one of our targets the angle of sight, properly so called, worked out at more than twenty degrees, while the map-range elevation was only about fifteen. The devising of an accurate formula for correction of elevation for a large " *dislivello*," as the Italians shortly call it, which in English means a large " difference of level " between a gun and its target, is one of the most intricate problems of theoretical gunnery, or, for that matter, of theoretical mechanics, involving, among other factors, the various shapes and sizes of projectiles, their comparative steadiness during flight, the resistance of the air, and the effect of other atmospheric conditions and of the force of gravity.

There was a splendid opportunity for systematically testing various rival formulæ in the Trentino, but it was allowed to slip. Among gunners, as among other classes, and especially among Regular Army gunners, the so-called practical man sees little value in scientific experiments, which do not produce large, obvious and quick returns. We fired many hundred rounds in the Trentino and I have no doubt that they were tolerably effective. But most of them were fired at night, with no observation possible, and we were often restricted in our registrations by daylight to four rounds a section per target, from which no really reliable conclusions could be drawn.[1]

.   .   .   .   .   .

We were billeted in the village of Tiarno di Sotto, where the Mayor under the Austrian régime, an Italian by race, was still carrying on his duties. " But I shall have to disappear, if the Austrians ever come back," he said with a smile. It was a tremendous climb from our billets to get anywhere, the least tremendous being to our Battery position, straight up the nearest mountain side. A very active and energetic man could get up in a quarter of an hour. It used to take me twenty minutes. The weather, moreover, was hot, though considerably cooler than on the plains.

Some Czecho-Slovaks were billeted in the next house to ours, but, owing to lack of a common language, we were unfortunately unable to talk to them. They were well-built fellows, and gave one an impression of great tenacity and intelligence. And I know that they were fine fighters. But they had not the gaiety of the Italians, partly perhaps because they were exiles in a strange land, and must so remain till the day of final victory, which might then have seemed still infinitely remote. An amusing incident happened one evening. Four officers had deserted from the Austrian lines and surrendered to the Czecho-Slovaks ; it was one of their military functions to induce surrenders. Two of these officers were themselves Czecho-Slovaks, the third a Jugo-Slav and the

---

[1] We could get no help from Italian range tables, which were not merely for different guns and ammunition, but were drawn up on different principles from our own.

fourth an Italian from Istria. They were very
hungry and were in the midst of a good meal, in the
presence of a Czecho-Slovak guard, when a Corporal
and two gunners from our Battery, passing outside
the house and hearing some language being spoken
within, which they recognised to be neither English
not Italian, rightly thought it their duty to enter and
investigate the matter. The deserters were astonished
to see these unfamiliar looking persons, speaking a
strange tongue and wearing a uniform which they
had never seen before. But they were still more
astonished to learn that they were British. They
seemed hardly to be aware that the British were at
war with Austria, much less that any British troops
had been within hundreds of miles of them. The
incident closed in much mirth and friendliness.

In the village were also billeted many Italian troops,
who used to fill the night with song, long after most
of us had gone to bed :—

> " ' Addio, mia bell', addio ! '
>   Cantava nel partir la gioventù,"

which is never very far from the lips of any Italian
soldier, and those endless *stornelli*, which to an invariable tune they multiply from day to day.

> " Il General Cadorna
>   Mangiava la bifstecca ;
>   Ai poveri soldati
>   Si dava castagna secca,"[1]

---

[1] " General Cadorna used to eat beefsteak. To the poor soldiers
they gave dried chestnuts."

or

> " Il Re dal fronte Giulio
>   Ha scritto alla Regina,
>   ' Arrivato a Trieste
>   Ti manderò una cartolina,' " [1]

with its sardonic variant or sequel,

> " Il General Cadorna
>   Ha scritto alla Regina
>   ' Se vuoi veder Trieste,
>   Compra una cartolina.' " [2]

Many of the others are for various reasons unprintable, though many are extremely witty and amusing. Even those which I have quoted were nominally forbidden by the High Command to be sung, but the prohibition was not very rigorously enforced. And General Cadorna, after all, had now passed into history. Of his successor I never heard any evil sung, though I remember once hearing a great crowd of soldiers and civilians at Genoa shouting monotonously.

> " Viva, viva il Generale Dia ! "

The refrain of the *stornelli* was onomatopœic, and was intended to represent the sound of gunfire.

> " Bim Bim Bom,
>   Bim Bim Bom,
>   Al rombo del cannon."

What a theatrical country Italy is ! I remember

[1] " The King has written to the Queen from the Julian Front, ' when I get to Trieste, I will send you a picture post card.' "

[2] " General Cadorna has written to the Queen, ' if you want to see Trieste, buy a picture post card.' "

HUTS ON A MOUNTAIN SIDE IN THE TRENTINO

being out in the streets of Tiarno one evening with a
stream of song issuing from almost every house, and
looking up at the full moon riding high over the
towering peaks that locked in our valley and all but
shut out the night sky. I could hardly believe that
it was neither a stage setting nor a dream.

I remember another day, when I did a great climb
above Bezzecca to carry out a front line reconnaissance,
and arrived limp and perspiring to lunch at the
Headquarters of an Italian Artillery Group, high,
high up, looking out upon a glorious and astounding
view. And in the afternoon I took my first ride on a
teleferica, or aerial railway, slung along a steel rope
across the deeps, seated on a sort of large wooden
tea tray, some six feet long and two and a half across,
with a metal rim some six inches high running round
the edge. I was quite prepared to be sick or at least
giddy. But I was pleasantly disappointed. My
journey took about a quarter of an hour ; walking it
would have taken about three hours of very stiff
climbing. The motion is quite steady, except for a
slight jolt as one passes each standard, and, provided
one sits still and doesn't shift one's centre of gravity
from side to side, there is no wobbling of the tea tray.
And looking down from time to time I saw tree tops
far below me, and men and mules on mountain tracks
as black specks walking.

.   .   .   .   .   .

There were various theories to account for our
being sent to the Trentino. One was that an Austrian
attack was feared there, another that an Italian
attack was intended, but that the intention was
afterwards abandoned, a third that the whole thing

was a feint to puzzle the Austrians. But in any case we did not remain there long. By the beginning of August we were back on the Plateau. On the return journey, which was again by road all the way, we were given three days' rest at Desenzano and I was able to spend half a day in Verona.

CHAPTER XXXIV

SIRMIONE AND SOLFERINO'

" LEAVE is a privilege and not a right," according to a hack quotation from the King's Regulations. This quotation has done good service in the mouth of more than one Under Secretary of State for War, heading off tiresome questioners in the British House of Commons. Leave was a very rare privilege for the British Forces in Italy. In France, taking a rough average of all ranks and periods, British troops got leave once a year. In my Battery in Italy, the majority were without leave home for nineteen months. How much longer they would have had to wait, if the war had not conveniently come to an end in the nineteenth month of their Italian service, I do not know. Even in Italy, of course, the privilege was extended somewhat more freely to junior regimental officers and much more freely to Staff officers and Lieutenant-Colonels, in view of the danger of brain fag and nervous strain following upon their greater mental exertions and their abnormal exposure to shell fire and the weather. The former class went home about every eleventh, the latter about every third month.

The French Parliament fairly early in the war, with that gross lack of discrimination and of military understanding habitual to politicians, insisted on the granting of leave every three months to all ranks in all theatres of war. The Italian Parliament pedantically laid down a uniform period of six months. The British Parliament, with the sure political instinct of our race, preferred to leave the whole matter in the hands of the War Office. The interference in purely military affairs of unpractical sentimentalists was strongly discouraged at Westminster.

Why no leave to England could be granted except in special cases, was cogently explained from time to time during the summer in circulars written by Staff officers of high rank, who had frequent opportunities of informing themselves of the realities of the situation, while visiting London. These circulars were read out on parade and treated with the respect which they deserved. To allay possible, though quite unreasonable, unrest, it was determined to open a British Club, or Rest Camp, at Sirmione, which, as every reader of Tennyson knows, stands on the tip of a long promontory at the southern end of Lake Garda. Here a week's holiday was granted to a large proportion of the officers and a small proportion of the rank and file. Many officers went there more than once. Two large hotels were hired, which had been chiefly frequented before the war by corpulent and diseased Teutons, for whom a special course of medical treatment, including sulphur baths, used to be prescribed.

One of these hotels was now set apart for British
officers, the other for men. A funny little person in
red tabs was put in charge ; there were various
speculations as to his past activities, but all agreed
that he had got into a good job now, and wasn't going
to lose it, if tact could prevent it. This little man
used to stand outside the hotel gates as each week's
guests arrived from the steamer, and always had a
cheery smile of welcome for every Field officer ; to
General officers he showed special attentions. He
took his meals in the same room as the rest of us,
but at what was known as " the Staff table," where
he invited to join him any officers of high rank, who
might be staying at the hotel, or, if there were none
such available, certain. of his private friends. The
food supplied to ordinary people like myself was good,
wholesome, reasonably plentiful and cheap. At " the
Staff table " special delicacies were provided and
additional courses, with no increase of charge. The
profits, he used to say, were made entirely on the
drinks and smokes.

A series of rules was drawn up, that none of us might
be led into any avoidable temptation. All towns
within reach,— Milan, Verona, Mantua, Brescia,
Peschiera,—were placed out of bounds. So, too,
were some of the larger villages on the shores of the
Lake. The hours during which alcoholic liquor might
be obtained, either in the Hotels or in the Cafés of
Sirmione, were narrowly limited. Beer was strictly
rationed. Carefully regulated excursions on the Lake,
by steamer or launch, were permitted and even
encouraged. Likewise bathing.

I spent a week here, from August 14th to 21st, in gloriously fine, hot weather. Some said that the damp heat was relaxing and depressing, but I, in my second Italian summer, was getting acclimatised. The place was wonderfully beautiful. The end of the promontory is covered with olive trees, the ground thickly carpeted with wild mint and thyme, surrounded on three sides by the deep blue water of the Lake, along the shores of which lie little white villages, backed by groups of straight, dark cypresses, with mountain ranges rising in the background, range behind range, and overhead the hot Italian sun, shining from a cloudless sky. Here, at the point, were the ruins of what are called, upon what evidence I know not, the Villa, the Baths and the Grotto of Catullus. Here, too, was an Italian Anti-Aircraft Battery, and the Grotto of Catullus was filled with their ammunition.

The Austrians still held the upper end of the Lake, including the town of Riva. But only Italian motor boats now survived on the Lake, occasionally raiding Riva. The Austrian boats had all been sunk early in the war.

. . . . . .

On the 15th I went round the lower end of the Lake in a steamer and, passing along the shores of the beautiful Isola di Garda, on which stands the less beautiful Villa Borghese, landed at Maderno, famous for its lemon groves. Here a church was being used as a ration store. It had fine carving on the door. The French had established Artillery and Machine Gun Schools close to the Lake and several of their officers were on the steamer.

On the 16th I went with a young officer from a

15

Yorkshire Battalion, a most agreeable companion, to Desenzano, which was out of bounds. We played billiards and lunched, and in the afternoon went to sleep on the grass in the shade beside the Lake. We were driven back in a carrozza along the promontory by an old Garibaldino, a Capuan by birth, who in 1860 at the age of eleven joined Garibaldi, when he crossed from Sicily to the mainland, and held older people's horses at the Battle of the Volturno. He served with the Fifth Garibaldini in the Trentino campaign of 1866 and knew intimately the country where I had lately been, the Val d'Ampola and Storo, Tiarno and Bezzecca. He then joined the Italian Regular Army, and in 1870 was a Corporal in the Pavia Brigade. He was present at the taking of Rome and claimed that, although an Infantryman, he helped to load one of the guns which breached the Porta Pia. If this claim be true, there must have been either a lack of gunners on this famous occasion, or a certain degree of enthusiastic confusion. Having entered Rome, he got very drunk and absented himself from his Regiment without leave for three days. As a punishment he was made to march on foot, carrying a full pack, from Rome to Padua. He showed us his old military pay-book, his medals and other souvenirs. Next year he will be seventy years old and will begin to draw a pension. Having returned to Sirmione, we arranged with him to drive us next day to the neighbouring battlefields of 1859, San Martino and Solferino. Much delighted, he assured me, quite without necessity, that next day he would put on his best clothes, would wash and shave, and give his horse an extra bit of grooming.

Accordingly next morning at ten o'clock we started off again in the carrozza. We visited first San Martino della Battaglia, only a few miles from the southern end of the Lake. This was the northern extremity of the battlefield of Solferino. It was here that the Sardinians and Piedmontese, forming the left wing of the Franco-Italian Army, ·attacked and drove back the Austrian right wing. A memorial tower has been erected here, 250 feet high, with great avenues of cypresses radiating outwards from it. The custodian is a handsome boy, who lost a leg at the taking of Gorizia two years ago. There is no staircase within the tower ; one goes up by a spiral inclined plane. At successive stages, as one ascends, are large and detailed paintings, running right round the inner circumference of the tower, representing the battles of the Italian Wars of Liberation from 1848 to 1870. As works of art they are not of the first class, but they convey here and there a vivid sense of life and movement, an advance of the Bersaglieri with their cocks' feathers waving in the wind, Garibaldini in their red shirts rushing Bomba's gunners on the Volturno, Italian cavalry charging a Battalion of brown-coated Croats at Custozza, the defence of a fort in the Venetian lagoons against Austrian warships.

On a fine day the view from the top is very good, but that day it was hazy in the great heat. Close by is an Ossario, containing the skulls and bones of seven thousand dead collected in the neighbourhood, washed clean with white wine and set out in neat rows, the majority Italian. A good warning, one would think, against war, and more compact and less wasteful of space than a conventional graveyard.

Thence we drove on to Solferino, a little remote
village with a single street paved with cobble stones,
seldom visited by foreign tourists. The plaster on the
walls of the farmhouses hereabouts still bears many
bullet marks. As we drove, the Garibaldino pointed
out to us some of the positions where Napoleon III.'s
Generals had sited their Batteries. We were the
first British officers seen here during the war, and
had an enthusiastic reception. I was surprised to
find that none of our Regulars had come over from
Sirmione, as a matter of professional interest and duty,
to study the tactics of 1859 upon the ground.

We lunched well at a small *albergo*. There were four
good-looking daughters of the house, who came and
sat with us in turn and watched us eat. They had
the naturalness and simple charm of dwellers in remote
places. "Four good cows," said the Garibaldino,
with the frank realism of the South, "but all the
local proprietors are too old." After lunch my
companion remained in the village, and I climbed
the ridge from which the French drove the Austrians,
a very strong natural position even now. I went up
La Rocca, at its south-eastern extremity, on which
stands an old square tower, also converted into a
battle memorial. Here again there are no steps
within, but an ascending spiral plane. The slopes
at this end of the ridge are thickly planted with
young cypresses, and the place will grow in beauty
year by year. Even now it is well wooded, with
larger trees just below the tower. The village lies
at the foot of the slope. Just outside it, off the road
on slightly rising ground at the end of an avenue,
is another and larger Ossario, containing twenty

thousand skulls and sets of bones, French and Austrian.
The building is full of banners and wreaths and
memorial tablets, including one lately sent by the
French troops now fighting on the Italian Front.

> " Ceux de la grande guerre
> A ses glorieux anciens.
> 1859–1918."

A few skeletons have been preserved intact, including
one said to have been an Austrian bandmaster, a
giant eight feet tall. The nationality of some of the
skulls can be determined by bullets, French or
Austrian, found in the head and now attached by a
string.

I stepped forth from this well-ordered tomb into
the outer sunshine with a sense of personal oppression
and of human ineffectiveness. How slowly and how
clumsily do the feet of History slouch along ! And
yet, if Napoleon III. had kept faith with Cavour, the
fighting here might have liberated Venetia without
the necessity for another war a few years later. How
quiet and silent lie these battlefields of yesterday !
Even so, one day, will lie the pine woods round Asiago,
shell-torn and tormented now, and populous with
the soldiers of many nations, yet of a wondrous
beauty in the full moonlight and the fresh night air.
I shall be back up there in three days' time !

.   .   .   .

We drove back in the warm evening, by the road
through Pozzolengo toward Peschiera, along which
many of the defeated Austrians fled in 1859. The
roadside was dusty, but along all the hedges the
acacias still showed a most delicate and tender green.

CHAPTER XXXV

THE ASIAGO PLATEAU ONCE MORE

DURING August and September we were kept pretty busy on the Plateau. Concentrations on enemy trenches and wire and special counter-battery shoots by day and counter-battery support of Infantry raids by night were continually required of us. We fired high explosive by day and chiefly gas shell at night. Our own Infantry and the French on our right raided the enemy's front and support lines very frequently, bringing back many prisoners. The French constantly penetrated and reconnoitred the enemy's defensive system on Mount Sisemol. Many of us were inclined to think that the casualties, sometimes heavy, which were incurred in these raids, and the great quantity of ammunition shot away, were largely wasted. We saw no sufficient return for them, beyond a certain amount of information obtained from prisoners, much of which was of small and doubtful value. But in view of what happened later, I think it must be agreed that these continual raids and bombardments did their share in gradually wearing down the morale and power of resistance of the Austrian Army.

There was a persistent rumour that the enemy was on the point of retiring to a line, on which he was known to be working hard, along the lower slopes of Monte Interrotto and Monte Catz on the far side of the Plateau. This line, we learned from prisoners, was commonly referred to as the *Winterstellung*

(winter position). It would have been stronger,
defensively, than his existing line, and would have
had the great advantage of being able largely to
be supplied and munitioned during daylight, as
there was much good cover and roads hidden in
the pine woods leading down immediately behind it.
It would have involved the moral disadvantage of
evacuating the ruins of Asiago. But, with the snow
down on the Plateau, every Austrian track and foot-
mark would have been visible from our O.P.'s, and
the Austrian situation, bad as it already was from
this point of view, would have become quite intolerable. If, on the other hand, we had followed up
an Austrian retreat to their *Winterstellung* by the
occupation of Asiago and the throwing forward of
our line across the Plateau, the relative situation
would have been reversed. Our Infantry and many
of our Batteries would then be out in the open, in
view from the Austrian O.P.'s, unable to light a fire
by day, and only able to send up supplies by night ;
and our general situation would be so much the worse
with heavy snow increasing our discomfort and the
visibility of any work we might undertake and of our
every movement.

For this reason, as has been explained in an earlier
chapter, it was taken for granted that a small advance
from our present excellent line would be worse than
useless, and that only an advance at least to the crest
of the first mountain range beyond the Plateau would
be of any military value. The possibility of such an
advance being attempted was evidently still in the
minds of the Staff, for our forward or Battle Position
at San Sisto had to be kept in constant readiness for

occupation, and it was suggested by some that the occasion for a big attack would be the moment when the enemy was in the act of retiring voluntarily to his *Winterstellung*, necessarily a somewhat difficult and risky operation.

Meanwhile the enemy guns were not silent. They were indeed unpleasantly active, constantly sweeping the road just behind our Battery, putting down violent, though brief, concentrations on the cross roads at Pria dell' Acqua, less than a hundred yards to our right, and apparently also endeavouring to carry out occasional counter-battery shoots after our own pattern. The British Batteries in this sector suffered a number of casualties during this period, and one in particular, not my own, was frequently shelled with great precision by twelve-inch howitzers, most disagreeable weapons, firing at extreme ranges from the cover of some distant valley. Many efforts were made to locate these particular guns, but I am not confident that any of them were successful. Among the victims in this Battery was Preece, a young officer who had served under me in a Training Battery in England. He was the only son of a widowed mother, and, had he lived, might have become a world-famous chemist. His grave, too, is in the Baerenthal Valley.

Our own officers' Mess had several narrow escapes, especially on one occasion when the impact of an enemy shell was broken by a trench cart and a box of tools, only seven or eight yards away. None of the tools were ever found again and portions of the trench cart were seen next morning hanging on the telephone wires beside the road. Only a few splinters came into the Mess and did no harm, all the occupants, myself included, warned by the sound of the approaching shell, having flung ourselves face downwards on the floor. Another frequent exercise of the enemy at this time was night bombing, which during the full moon became somewhat serious. But a big raid by our own airmen on the enemy aerodrome at Borgo in the Val Sugana put an end to this source of trouble.

I was able now and then to make short expeditions down the mountains in the Battery car to Thiene, and sometimes even to Vicenza, for the ostensible purpose of buying canteen and mess stores and drawing the Battery pay. Thiene is the ugliest and dullest little town in Italy. But Vicenza, with its exquisite Olympian theatre, and other fine Palladian architecture, varied by many smaller buildings which are beautiful examples of the Venetian Gothic style, with its busy and animated Piazza, centring round the ever-crowded Café Garibaldi, and with the wooded slope of the famous Monte Berico, rich with historic memorials, rising behind the town, never failed to lift my mind out of the dreary monotony of war into an atmosphere of cleaner and more enduring things. I remember, too, the strange thrill I had one day, when, having passed the sawmills and dumps of stores and shells and the huddle of Headquarter offices at Granezza, I came out on the last edge of the mountain wall, into sudden full view of the great plain below, full of rivers and cities, and saw, for the first time from up here, the sunlight flashing on a strip of distant golden sea. It was the lagoons round Venice.

I spent also many interesting days about this time at our tree O.P. on Cima del Taglio. The Italians had an O.P. in a neighbouring tree, which they called Osservatorio Battisti. The British Field Artillery occupied a third tree, and the French a fourth. The pine trees on that summit were, literally, full of eyes. But the enemy never discovered any of us, though he sometimes dropped a few stray shells in our neighbourhood. Our own O.P. was not generally manned at night, unless some prearranged operation was taking place, but the officer on duty had to remain within call and slept in a log hut near the foot of the tree, in telephonic communication with Battery and Brigade.   The French and Italians also had huts close by, and I spent several evenings playing chess with them, or talking, or listening to the mandolin and the singing of Italian *stornelli*. One young Italian, in particular, I remember with some affection, a certain Lieutenant Prato, a mandolin player of great skill and a very charming personality.

One day in September, when the news from the French Front was getting better and better, I remember talking, on our tree top, to the Italian officer, who was at that time acting as *liaison* officer to our Brigade, a member of a family well known in Milan. He knew every inch of those mountains, now in Austrian hands, along the old Italian frontier. His Battery had fought there in the early part of the war. He knew, too, Gorizia and the Carso battlefields. And he was sick at heart, as every Italian always silently was, at the memory of the retreat of last autumn. And I remember saying that what was now happening in the Somme country would happen

soon in Italy. There, I reminded him, was a stretch
of country which we had once conquered, inch by inch,
with terrible losses and infinite heroism and insufficient
Artillery, just as Italy had conquered those positions
on the Carso and on Monte Santo. And all those
gains of ours had been wiped out in a few disastrous
hours last March, as Italy's had been wiped out last
October, and now we were advancing again over that
same country and beyond it, far more rapidly and
with far smaller losses than in those bloody days two
years ago. And so, I prophesied to him, would it be
on this Front too. The day was coming when Italy
would win back all she had lost, and far more than
she had ever won before, far more swiftly and cheaply
than in her early brave offensives, and Austria, like
Germany, would be broken in hopeless, irretrievable
defeat. He said to me then that he hoped it might
come true, but that he was less certain of the future
than I. But, two months later, when I had proved
to be a true prophet, he reminded me of that conversation of ours.

PART VI

THE LAST PHASE

CHAPTER XXXVI

THE MOVE TO THE PIAVE

THE second week in October we moved down from the Plateau and lay for a week at Mestre, within sight of Venice. One clear afternoon it looked as though one could throw a stone across the intervening water. Every one took for granted that a big Italian offensive was imminent. The rumour was that it would be timed to begin, as near as possible, on the anniversary of the defeat of Caporetto. In Italy more weight is attached to anniversaries than with us. One felt expectation everywhere in the air.

It was during these days that I fell in with the Rumanian Legion. I had been in Padua and saw a group of them standing on the platform at the railway station. They were obviously not Italians. Their uniform was similar to that of the Italian Infantry, but their collars were red, yellow and blue, and they wore a cockade of the same three colours on their hats. They wore Sam Browne belts, too, and carried a *pugnale* like the Italian Arditi. I asked a Carabiniere on duty who they were. He smiled but did not know. " Perhaps Yugo-Slavs," he suggested. One of them overheard our conversation and came up to me saying, " Siamo Rumeni, Legione Rumena." Then followed a tremendous fraternisation. We shook hands all round and began to talk. We talked Italian, which, being very like their own language, they all understood. Indeed, for an Italian Rumanian is much easier to understand than many of the Italian local dialects.

They were attractive people, of all ages and very friendly, rather like Italians, but with a queer indescribable racial difference. They were natives, mostly, of Transylvania and had much to say of the oppression of their nationality by the Magyars. Most of them had been conscribed to fight in the Austro-Hungarian Army, but had crossed over to the Italian lines at the first opportunity. One said, " There are four millions of us in Austria and Hungary." Then, with an air of restrained fury, " Is that not enough ? " Another said, " But after the war there will be a Great Rumania —great and beautiful." And another said, " We Rumanians must be very grateful to Guglielmone.[1] If he had not made this war, we should not have seen the Greater Rumania in our lifetime. But now, if it was not certain before, the blunders of Carluccio [2] have put it beyond all doubt." And another told me that his father wrote and spoke English very well, having lived for twelve years in America at St Louis. And another explained to me how the Rumanians had retained, more than any other modern nation, the speech and customs and dress and traditions of

[1] " Big William."   [2] " Wretched little Charles."

the ancient Romans, which things they had originally
derived from the legionaries of the Emperor Trajan.[1]
When we parted I said, " May we all meet again on
the field of victory beyond the Piave. Long live
the Greater Rumania ! " And they all cried, " Long
live England ! Long live victory ! " And so I was
going away, when one of them, a little fellow, with
a rather sad, earnest face, who had apparently missed
a parting handshake, ran after me about twenty
yards, and seized me by the hand and cried again,
" Long live victory ! "

.   .   .   .   .

From Mestre we moved up through Treviso to a
Battery position, on which an advance party had
been at work for several days. It grew more and
more certain that the offensive was coming at last.
Troops of all arms were moving forward in unending
streams along every road leading toward the Piave.
Prominent among them were many Italian Engineers
and bridging detachments with great numbers of
pontoons. Beyond Treviso all troop movements
took place at night, and our defensive (and offensive)
measures against aircraft were apparently sufficient
to prevent the enemy from getting any clear idea of
what was going on. It seems that he expected an
attack in the mountains, but not on the plain. The
Italian High Command, on the other hand, considered
that the relative strength and morale of the opposing
Armies was now such that we could attack on the

[1] This common boast of the Rumanians is quite true. It is
partly to be accounted for by the fact that they were able to retreat
before successive invading hordes of barbarians into the inaccessible
valleys of the Carpathians, and come down again on to the plains
when the danger had passed by.

plain without fear of a successful counter-attack in
the mountains, and that, the attack on the plain
once well under way, we could pass to the offensive
in the mountains also. This view of things was
justified by the events which followed. Two British
Divisions were moved down to the plain, and one
was left in the mountains. The Heavy Artillery was
divided proportionately and, of my own Brigade, one
Battery was left in the mountains but the rest moved
down.

Our new Battery position lay between the ruined
village of Lovadina and the river Piave, about three-
quarters of a mile from the nearer bank. There was
a farmhouse, not much knocked about, close to the
gun pits and, with the aid of a few tents erected
out of sight along a shallow ditch, the whole Battery
was very tolerably billeted. Another British Battery
was less than a hundred yards in rear of us, and two
others not far away on our right flank. We were once
more in a land of acacia hedges, beginning now to
take on their autumn tints. For miles round us the
country was dead flat. Beyond the river we could
see, on a little rise, what was left of Susegana Castle,
near to Conegliano, and on a higher, longer ridge
further away the white *campanile* of San Daniele
del Friuli, above Udine. It was there that, almost
a year ago, in the first newspaper I saw after the
retreat, I had read that Italian rearguards were still
fighting. In the far distance rose great mountain
masses. Up there were Feltre and Belluno, and
behind, just visible when the light was very bright,
the peaks of Carnia and the Cadore.

It was an unaccustomed feeling, after months of

comparative immunity from observation behind mountain ridges, to be in flat country again. At first we all felt a queer sense of insecurity whenever we walked about, even when thick hedges manifestly screened us from enemy eyes. But the road from Lovadina to the river bank at Palazzon, which ran right through our position and within a few yards of our billet, was in full view, and no movement along it was permitted during daylight. When we first arrived we found a deep sense of gloom prevailing amongst our advanced party. They were convinced that our position had been spotted already, for the Austrians that morning had put down a five minutes' concentration all round the place. Nothing much heavier than Field Guns had been firing, but it had been lively while it lasted. It seemed probable, however, on further inquiry, that this outburst had been caused by the fact that an idiotic officer belonging to the Battery immediately in rear of us had marched a working party up the road in fours, then halted them and allowed the men to stand about in groups on the road for several minutes. It was at these groups that the Austrians had apparently been firing. A vigorous protest extracted from our neighbours a promise that more common sense should be used in future.

We were to remain a silent Battery until the start of the offensive, and this was to be dependent on the height of the river, which at that time was in, full flood owing to heavy rains in the mountains. Our guns were well camouflaged and the chances of our detection seemed small. But one day we had a lucky escape. It was very clear and there had been great activity in the air on both sides all the morning. All seemed quiet again, however, and we had the camouflage off one of our guns, and two small parties working in the open on shelter trenches behind. A plane was seen approaching, but the air sentry, whose duty it was to keep a sharp look out through glasses and signal the approach of enemy aircraft by two blasts of a whistle, gave no warning. He had been deceived by the marking on the plane, a very thin black cross instead of the thick one usually found on enemy aircraft. Not till it was right upon us did he blow the whistle, and then it was too late. The plane flew very low over us. We could see the pilot looking calmly down at our uncovered gun, and our men trying, ineffectually and belatedly, to take cover. He certainly took it all in and marked us down on his map. The position was very easy to identify owing to the solitary farmhouse and the road close by. A few rifle shots were fired, but they did him no harm, and he sailed away toward the river and his own lines.

We had certainly been spotted. And then we suddenly saw another plane, this time an Italian, coming from the left, flying high, hard in pursuit. The Austrian began to rise, but the Italian outpaced him and got right above him, and pressed him gradually down towards the ground. We heard the wooden-sounding *clack-clack-clack* of machine gun fire. And then we saw the Austrian evidently go out of control, diving toward the ground, more and more rapidly, and the Italian circling downwards above him; and then the Austrian went out of sight behind the acacias and a few moments later a column of smoke began to

16

rise.   He had crashed in flames, just this side of the
river, and his valuable information with him.   The
Italian flew back over us, triumphantly and very low
this time, and waved his hand to us. And we gave
him a grateful cheer.

CHAPTER XXXVII

THE BEGINNING OF THE LAST BATTLE

BY the night of October 24th the river had fallen
a few inches, and British Infantry crossed in
small boats to the Grave di Papadopoli, a long
island of sand in the middle of the stream.   On the
right a Battalion of the Gordons crossed, rowed over by
Venetian boatmen.   I met one of their officers afterwards. " Everyone of those boatmen deserved a
decoration," he said. " They were all as cool under
heavy shell fire as if they had been rowing on the
Grand Canal."   Our Infantry held their preliminary
positions here for two days, in spite of considerable
Austrian bombardment and counter-attacks.   British
aeroplanes flew over the island and dropped rations
in sandbags.   Throughout the fighting of these two
days, we were standing by ready to open fire, if
orders should come.   But no orders came and we
remained a silent Battery.

But on the night of October 26th, half an hour
before midnight, the big bombardment opened and
our guns spoke again.   It was to be their last great
oration.   It was, of its kind, a fine, thunderous per-

formance, and the Austrian reply, in our own
neighbourhood, was feeble. Evidently they had not
spotted our position, thanks to that Italian airman.
Our targets were enemy Batteries and Brigade Headquarters. We fired gas shells continuously for many
hours, switching from one target to another, until a
strong wind got up, rendering gas shelling compara-
tively ineffective. Then we got orders to change
to high explosive. The gun detachments worked
splendidly, as always. We were below strength and
could not furnish complete reliefs, but no one spared
himself or grumbled.

On the morning of the 27th, just before 7 o'clock,
our Infantry attacked, crossing from the island to the
further bank of the river. There were no bridges,
and the water was breast high in some places. In
places it came right over the heads of the smaller men,
but their taller comrades pulled them through. Where
the current was strongest, cables were thrown across
and firmly secured, and to these men held on, as
they forced their passage through the water.

About ten o'clock I went forward from the Battery
position to the river bank at Palazzon to ascertain
the situation. A little man named Sergeant Barini,
half an Italian and half an Englishman, but serving
in the English Army and attached to our Battery,
accompanied me. At Palazzon the river was broad
and, under fire, unbridgeable, and we went half a
mile down stream along what up to this morning had
been our front line trench, to the bridgehead at
Lido Island. The islands in mid stream were crowded
with prisoners and wounded coming back and fresh
troops going forward, and dead bodies lay about,

British and Austrian together, of men who had fought their last fight, and two crashed aeroplanes. The Austrians had put up elaborate barbed-wire defences on the island, but these had been pretty well broken up by our fire.

Some enemy guns of big calibre were still shelling the crossings and causing casualties among a Battalion of the Northumberland Fusiliers, who were in reserve, waiting on the bank for the order to cross. I tried to locate as accurately as possible the direction of these guns and reported them by telephone to our Brigade Headquarters. I saw an Infantry Brigadier, who said that things were going well, but asked for some additional Artillery support for his left flank on the other side, and, if possible, for an enemy Battery, which he thought was near Susegana Castle, to be knocked out. I looked across the river and saw the dense white smoke screen which our Field Guns were putting up to cover the advance.

These Italian rivers of the Venetian Plain, fed by the melting Alpine snows, are not at all like the Thames. Where I was, there were about nine successive channels, varying in breadth and depth, and in between, stones and sand and rough vegetation on islands varying in size and shape and number with the height of the river. And it was no uncommon thing for the river to rise or fall several feet in a night, for whole islands to be submerged, or for whole channels to run dry. The difficulty here of carrying out military operations according to a time table arranged several days in advance was very great.

Over the main channels pontoons had been thrown, over others light plank bridges, less strongly supported,

through others everybody was wading. Large bodies
of Engineers, mostly Italian, were ceaselessly working
at these river crossings, and working magnificently.
For not only was it necessary to be constantly
strengthening and multiplying the bridges already
made, to take the ever-increasing volume of traffic that
would be required to supply the troops across the
river, but the enemy's guns were still firing with
terrible accuracy at the crossings, and swarms of
enemy planes were constantly appearing, bombing
the bridges and the islands in a last desperate effort
to hold up our advance. Our planes, too, were never
far away, and succeeded in driving off or driving down
many of these attackers. But others got through and
were constantly undoing the work of the Engineers.

When we had got all the information we could,
Barini and I went back to the Battery and reported
what we had heard and seen. On the way I let
myself go and spouted much cheap rhetoric, I am
afraid, at the little man. And he laughed rather
nervously and thought me, I expect, a queer companion in rather unpleasant surroundings. For
several shells kicked up great clouds of earth and
stones pretty close to us. But he too, I know, smelt
victory in the air that day.

CHAPTER XXXVIII

ACROSS THE RIVER

NEXT day I went over the river and right on, one of the two F.O.O.'s (forward observation officers) from my Brigade who were to establish and maintain contact with the advancing Infantry. Three signallers and a runner came with me, carrying rifles, bayonets and ammunition, a day's rations and much signalling gear. The other officer had his own party. We soon subdivided our work and separated.

The twenty-four hours of my duty do not lend themselves to a sustained description. I passed and identified from the map one of the targets of my Battery in the preliminary bombardment, an Austrian Battery position, which we had bombarded for many hours with gas and high explosive alternately. Our shooting had been accurate and deadly. The position was a mass of shell holes. One of the guns had been blown up, a second badly damaged. A third had been pulled out of its pit and half way up a bank by a team of horses. The enemy had made a desperate effort to get it away. But horses and men and fragments of men lay dead around it. It was a well prepared position, and well concealed by trees. But Italian airmen had spotted it, and marked it down with precision on the map, marked it down for destruction. The enemy had done much work here. There were fine, deep dug-outs, well timbered and weatherproof, comfortable dwelling places in

quiet times and strong enough to resist shell splinters
and even direct hits by guns of small calibre. But
we had got a direct hit on one dug-out and killed
half a dozen occupants. And the others had not
been proof against our gas. They were full of corpses,
mostly victims of gas. Some were wearing their gas
masks, but our gas had gone through them. Some
had apparently been gassed outside, some with
masks on and some without, and had crawled, dying,
into the dug-outs in the vain hope of finding pro-
tection there. However hardened one may grow,
by usage, to the common facts of war, few can look
on such a sight as this, without feeling a queer thrill
of very mixed emotion. My men looked with solemn
faces at the work they had helped to do. One said,
" poor chaps, *they* were pretty well done in ! " And
then we turned and went on.

.   .   .   .   .   .

It was a very rapidly moving warfare that day.
One Infantry Brigade Headquarters, with whom I
kept in intermittent touch, occupied four successive
positions, miles apart, in the course of twelve hours.
About noon I came to a ruined village, Tezze. I went
on to reconnoitre it with one signaller. In a half
wrecked house we heard the voices of Italian peasant
women and saw through an open door an ugly, little,
dirty child, probably about a year old, crawling among
rubbish and refuse. The village was only just ours.
On the far side of it men of the Manchester Regiment
were lining a ditch, under cover of a hedge, waiting
the order to charge. They warned me to go no
further along the road which, they said, was under
enemy machine gun fire. Every few minutes enemy

shells whistled over our heads and burst in the fields
and houses behind us. A wet wind blew down
the road. There was no fixed, clearly marked
line. Everything was in movement and rather
uncertain. . . .

Enemy guns, captured with their ammunition,
swung round and firing at the enemy, big guns and
little guns. . . .

On the British left the Como Brigade were advancing
rapidly in spite of pretty strong opposition. For a
while our left flank had been perilously in the air,
but the danger was past now. . . .

All the roads were thick with Austrian equipment
thrown away in the confusion of departure, rifles, steel
helmets (grotesquely shaped, like high-crowned
bowler hats), ammunition, coats, packs (handsomely
got up, with furry exteriors), mail bags, maps, office
stores, tin despatch boxes, photographs of blonde
girls, bayonets, hand bombs, . . . everything dead
thrust into the ditches, both men and horses, the latter
smelling earlier and stronger than the former. (The
more I look at dead bodies, the more childish and
improbable does the old idea of personal immortality
appear to me !) . . .

At one cross-roads a huge pool of blood, mingling
with and overwhelming the mud. Here a whole
transport team of heavy grey horses with wagons
had been hit and blown up. Close by, in a ditch,
two British wounded lay on stretchers, covered with
blankets. One, only lightly wounded, gave us information and directions. The other was very near
to death. His face was growing pale already, as
only the faces of the dead are pale. He was shifting

feebly and ineffectually, with the vain instinct to escape from pain. He was past speech, but he looked at us out of wide open half-frightened eyes that seemed to question the world despairingly, like an animal, broken helplessly in a trap. . . .

There were some civilians wandering on the roads, liberated now but uncertain whither to go or what place was safe, their possessions on carts. But soon the storm of battle will have passed well beyond them and they will be able to return to what is left of their homes. One old woman in black, walking lame, asked me if the Austrians would come back, and began to cry. I heard some of our soldiers saying in wonder to each other, " did you see those civies going along the road just now ? " Queer, irrelevant creatures in the battle zone ! . . .

Others, more fixed, liberated in their own villages, were eager to talk and to welcome us, but a little lost with the British and their unfamiliar ways and language, full of tales of the lack of food under the Austrian occupation, and the robbery of all their livestock and metal and many other things. But the retreat hereabouts had been too rapid and involuntary for deliberate burning or destruction or trap-setting on an appreciable scale. . . .

That night I made my headquarters in a wrecked church, from the tower of which I sent back signals in the morse code by means of a lamp. I slept for an hour or two under an Austrian blanket, none too clean as it afterwards appeared, and drank Austrian coffee and ate Austrian biscuits. . . .

All through that day and night and the day following the cannonading continued, but with very variable intensity at different points and times. Sometimes a tremendous affair, heavies, field guns and trench mortars all pounding away together, creeping barrage, smoke screens and the rest of it. Elsewhere and at other times, nothing, Infantry well ahead of the guns, going forward almost into the blue, with nothing heavier than machine guns to support them.

British Cavalry went through in the dawn, spectral, artistically perfect, aiming at ambitious, distant objectives, Northamptonshire Yeomanry who had come from France to Italy a year ago and had been kept behind the lines all through the war and were having their first show at last. The next day they suffered many casualties, but they did fine work. Their reconnaissance officer came into the church soon after midnight and asked me if the Austrians still held any part of the village. I told him no, not since yesterday morning.

.   .   .   .   .

Later on in the morning great masses of Infantry moved up through the village ; British Infantry with a look of evident satisfaction in their faces, but un-emotional ; Italian Infantry, looking usually even less expressive, but ready to burst into electrical enthusiasm at a touch, at a word, at a sign. . . . A British General, all smiles, rode past on his horse and stopped to ask me a question or two. He tapped me playfully on the helmet with his riding crop. " When will you get your guns across the river ? " he asked. " As soon, Sir, as the Sappers can build a bridge that will carry them," I replied. . . .

Now and again Italian planes going on, or coming back from, raids and reconnaissances, flying very

low over our heads, the pilots waving their hands over
the side and cheering, the troops on the roads cheering
back and upwards in return. . . .

When I was relieved, I tramped back to the Piave,
many miles now, and wading those of the channels
that were still unbridged returned, tired and footsore
but with a song in my heart, to my Battery.

.   .   .   .   .   .

Not till later did we come to comprehend the vast
sweep and the triumphantly executed plan of this
Last Great Battle.[1]

At dawn on the 24th, the same day that the British
Divisions had crossed to the Grave di Papadopoli,
the Italian Fourth Army had attacked in the Grappa
sector, where fighting was desperate and progress
slow for several days. On the evening of the 26th the
Piave was bridged in three sectors, and on the 27th
three bridgeheads were in being ; the first on the
Upper Piave, in the hands of Alpini and French
Infantry of the Italian Twelfth Army ; the second
on the Middle Piave, in the hands of Arditi and other
troops of the Italian Eighth Army ; the third further
downstream, in the hands of our two British Divisions
and the Italian Eleventh Corps. For a while the
situation had been critical owing to the gap between
the second and third bridgeheads. But by the
28th fresh Divisions had crossed the river at all three
bridgeheads, and spread out fanwise, linking up the
gaps in the line. The same day on the Asiago Plateau
the enemy at last fell hurriedly back to his *Winter-*

---

[1] For a full and lucid account see the official *Report by the
Comando Supremo on the Battle of Vittorio Veneto, 24th October—
2nd November* 1918.

stellung, and British troops occupied the ruins of Asiago itself.   During the next two days the advancing troops on the plain swept steadily eastwards.   On the 31st the enemy's line in the Grappa Sector completely collapsed, with great losses of men and guns.   On the 1st of November an attack was launched along the whole of the Italian Front, from the sea to the heights of the Stelvio, amid the glaciers and the eternal snows on the Swiss frontier, and on this day Italian, British and French troops carried at last, after strong resistance, the whole northern ridge of the Asiago Plateau, at which we had gazed with eyes of desire for many long months.

CHAPTER XXXIX

LIBERATORI

ON November the 1st a reconnaissance by car was ordered, to test the practicability and the need of accelerating the forward movement of our guns.   Leary and I and two others started early in a car, adequately armed and carrying a day's rations and a flask in which rum had been mixed accidentally with *florio* (marsala).   This most original mixture, which we christened " florium," was excellent, more thirst-quenching than rum, more sustaining to the spirit than florio.

That day we travelled 76 miles at the least, in a great curve, through liberated country.   We had everywhere an astounding reception, never to be

LORRIES LEAVING ASIAGO AFTER ITS LIBERATION

AUSTRIAN GUNS IN VAL D'ASSA CAPTURED BY BRITISH 48TH DIVISION

forgotten. Everywhere we passed, we were wildly, deliriously, cheered by the civilian population. Old men ran up to us waving their hats, old women clapped their hands, young girls waved and threw flowers at us, little boys ran shouting after us, all crying " Evviva ! Evviva ! Liberatori ! Viva gl' Inglesi ! " The radiant joy of them, and their smiles, never far from tears, were the manifestation of a form of human emotion, singularly pure and indescribably moving. Every town and village was hung with the Italian flag, and at one place an arch of flowers ran from tree to tree above the road. Everywhere crowds with smiling, wondering faces, stood watching the Allied troops moving up along the roads, wave upon wave upon wave, triumphant, unendingly. Here a few days ago the foreign invader had ruled, perhaps only yesterday, perhaps only a few hours ago. Now he had vanished, like a bad dream from which one suddenly awakes, leaving behind him only his dead, and certain grim marks of his occupation, and vivid memories of many brutal and cruel and thoughtless acts, to prove that he was worse and more real than a dream.

.   .   .   .   .   .

We crossed the Piave at Spresiano, on a series of wooden bridges and pontoons, similar to those further down the stream at Palazzon and Lido Island. On the further bank we came first to Conegliano. Here just a year ago some of von Below's German troops, who broke the line at Caporetto, had been billeted, and later a Bulgarian Governor and staff had been installed, for the encouragement and flattery of the wavering minor allies of the enemy powers. On the same principle a Turkish Governor had been appointed at Feltre. The troops of occupation had been guilty of wicked excesses at Conegliano. The little town had been ruthlessly ravaged and set on fire and the majority of the houses had been completely burnt out, only the charred shells of them remaining.

Hence we turned northwards up into the Alpine foothills, through country of exceptional beauty, and along the shores of a piece of long blue water, to the village of Revine Lago. Here were many captured and abandoned Austrian guns. Some, in the last desperate moments of departure, had been thrown down a steep cliff which overhangs the lake, and lay below us, for the time being out of reach. Here I met again several officers of the Italian Field Artillery, whom I met above Val Brenta in January, including the Neapolitan Adjutant of Colonel Bucci. Also General Clerici of the Bersaglieri, who for the moment had his Headquarters here, a friend of one of my companions. They all substantiated the rumour that last night, or the night before, Austrian envoys had appeared with a white flag in the Val Lagarina and had been taken to Diaz's Headquarters.

We parted from our friends and sped on to Vittorio Veneto, which gives its name to this last great battle, being the point on which those Italian forces moved, whose purpose and whose successful achievement it was to cut the Austrian Armies in two, separating the Armies in the mountains from the Armies in the plain. Vittorio stands on and around the summit of a little hill, itself one of the foothills, the older part of the town picturesque with little winding streets, the newer part well laid out with broad roads, shaded

with avenues of trees. Here the Austrian flight had
been more rapid and the damage smaller. But we
were still many miles behind the ever advancing battle
line. We determined, therefore, to turn sharply
eastward and make for Pordenone, in the hope of
coming up with the fighting thereabouts. For last
night, we heard, the Austrians were still defending
themselves on the near side of that town.

The road from Vittorio to Sacile grew thicker with
advancing troops, at first all Italian, then, as we
approached Sacile, mixed Italian and British, much
Italian Cavalry and Artillery, then British Infantry
and some Batteries of Field Guns. In Sacile itself,
which British troops had liberated, the crush of
troops was dense, and held us up for more than half
an hour. Union Jacks hung out from many houses,
side by side with the Italian tricolour. As we waited
for a chance to go forward, a Battalion of the Bisagno
Brigade went past along the side of the road, two
deep, at a steady double. Several officers I recognised,
whom I had met at dinner at a little restaurant at
Marostica many months before, and again near Casa
Girardi on the Plateau. We waved to one another
and cheered as they passed. When at last we moved
on again, we found the road from Sacile to Pordenone
pretty clear for several miles and were able to get
up speed. But what a sight this road presented !
Along it a confused mass of Austrian transport was
moving yesterday in headlong retreat. They were
bombarded by Artillery, ceaselessly bombed and
machine-gunned from the air. The slaughter here
had been great, the ditches were full of dead men
and horses, and the loss in wrecked and abandoned

material of every kind had been immense. And the civilians, who had been practically without food for many days, had been cutting up and eating the dead horses. " Poverini ! " said an Italian officer to whom we gave a lift into Pordenone, " they are all starving and we have little chance yet to bring them food."

Pordenone was ours. It had fallen in the early hours of this morning, but the departing Austrians had burnt and wrecked it. The streets were full of the débris and furniture which they had thrown out of the houses and shops in the last mad search for loot. We pushed on, and came up with British Infantry advancing, and the transport wagons and the steaming field cookers of two Battalions, and some cyclist companies of Bersaglieri. But the transport was at a standstill and the dismounted men only going forward slowly. We soon discovered the cause. The wooden bridge over the Meduna river was on fire, pouring forth clouds of smoke. The Austrians had been here only four hours before and had blown up two spans as they retreated and soaked the rest with paraffin and set it alight. The bridge was effectually destroyed. Italian Cavalry, we heard, had gone through the water in pursuit, and likewise some British Infantry patrols, swimming and wading and making use of various ingenious, improvised devices. But the Austrian had a good three hours start, and was running fast and travelling light, it was thought.

But we, being unable to get our car across, turned northward along the river bank and drove furiously and, after a mile or two, outran the foremost Infantry patrols (I think, of the Royal Warwicks), who were pushing cautiously forward, searching the woods and farmhouses for lurking rearguards. And so it was that, first of all the Allied troops, we four entered the little village of Nogaredo. And, as we came in, we sang, very loudly and perhaps somewhat out of tune, the chorus of *La Campana di San Giusto*, the forbidden song which to the Italian Irredentists stands for somewhat the same officially repressed but inextinguishable emotions, as that once forbidden song *The Wearing of the Green* stood for to the Nationalist Irishmen of a now vanished generation.

> " Le ragazze di Trieste
> Cantan tutte con ardore,
> ' O Italia, O Italia del mio core,
> Tu ci vieni a liberar ! ' " [1]

So to that village *we* were the visible liberators. All the villagers came running towards us, crowding around our car, weeping and cheering, pouring out their stories, touching and holding and kissing us. It is seldom that things happen with such dramatic perfection.

The last Austrians, they said, had been gone only half an hour. We pressed on along a narrow road, but it was late afternoon, and the light was failing. The road grew worse, and the mud thicker. Much retreating traffic had only lately traversed it. At last we stuck deep in two muddy ruts. The wheels skidded round helplessly. We could go neither forward nor backward. Three of us got out and shoved with all our strength. There was a crackle

---

[1] All the maidens of Trieste sing with passion, " O Italy, O Italy of my heart, thou comest to set us free ! "

of rifle shots not far away. We were prepared for an encounter. But nothing came of it. We got the car out at last, but the road was too bad for further progress and it was almost dark. We turned and drank up the remains of our " florium " and came back. But that day had been unforgettable.

CHAPTER XL

THE COMPLETENESS OF VICTORY

THE end was almost come. On November 3rd we received the official announcement that an armistice had been signed, and that at 3 p.m. on November 4th hostilities on the Italian-Austrian Front would cease. That same day Trento, Trieste and Udine fell. One began to be aware of the completeness of victory. On this day and the days that followed the communiqués of Diaz were decisive and historical.

" November 4th. Noon. The war against Austria-Hungary which . . . the Italian Army, inferior in numbers and resources, undertook on the 24th of May, 1915, and with unconquerable faith and stubborn valour conducted uninterruptedly and bitterly for 41 months, has been won. The great battle begun on the 24th October, in which there took part 51 Italian Divisions, 3 British, 1 French, 1 Czecho-Slovak and 1 American Regiment against 73 Austrian Divisions, is finished. . . . The Austrian Army is annihilated. It has suffered very heavy losses in the fierce resistance of the first days of the struggle and in the pursuit ; it has lost immense quantities of material of every kind and almost all its magazines and depôts ; it has left in our hands, up to the present, about 300,000 prisoners with complete staffs and not less than 5000 guns.[1] The remnants of what was once one of the most powerful Armies in the world are now flowing back in disorder and without hope up the mountain valleys down which they came with proud self-assurance."

" November 4th, 4 p.m. According to the conditions of the armistice . . . hostilities by land, sea and air on all the fronts of Austria-Hungary have been suspended at 3 p.m. to-day."

" November 6th. At 3 p.m. on the 4th of November our troops had reached Sluderno in the Val Venosta, the Pass of Mendola and the Defile of Salomo in the Val d'Adige, Cembra in the Val d'Avisio, Levico in the Val Sugana, Fiera di Primiero, Pontebba, Plezzo, Tolmino, Gorizia, Cervignano, Aquileia and Grado."

Some of these names filled me with memories of a year, and more than a year, ago. Old Natale's message to the enemy chalked on our hut at Pec had come true. We had soon come back.

. . . . . .

The fighting was over ! That night of the 4th of November all the sky was lit up with bonfires and the firing of coloured rockets and white Véry lights. One could hear bells ringing in the distance, back toward Treviso, and singing and cheering everywhere. It was an hour of perfection, and of accomplishment ;

[1] These figures increased later to more than 430,000 prisoners and 6800 guns.

17*

it was the ending of a story.   An epic cycle of history was finished, the cycle of the wars of Italy against Austria.   The task of completing Italian unity was finished, so far as a series of wars could finish it.

> " The fight is done, but the banner won ;
>   Thy comrades of old have borne it hence,
>   Have borne it in triumph hence.
>   Then the soldier spake from the deep, dark grave :
>   ' I am content.' "

The soldier had done his duty, now let the states-man do no less.   Let wisdom and imagination make sure the fruits of valour.

.   .   .   .   .   .

The old Austria is dead, and from her grave, which Italian hands have dug, are rising up new nations, the future comrades of the old nations and of Italy, who in these bloody years has grown from youth to full manhood.   It has been said that a nation is a friend-ship, and the common life of nations in the future must also be a friendship, necessarily less intimate but in no way less real.   The youth of the world must never be called to swim again, with old age on its back, through seas of needless death to the steep and distant cliffs of military victory.   There must be no more secret plots, nor seeming justification of plots, by little groups of elderly men against the lives and happiness of young men everywhere.   The world must be made safe for justice and for youth.

.   .   .   .   .   .

Youth was rejoicing that night in Italy, when the war against Austria ended.   And not youth only, nor Italians only.   The British troops loudly and healthily

and almost riotously sang also, all the temporary
soldiers and nearly all the regulars. Yet here and
there were gloom, and drab, wet blankets, trying to
make smoulder those raging fires of joy. In a few
officers' Messes, especially among the more exalted
units, men of forty years and more croaked like ravens
over their impending loss of pay and rank, Brigadier
Generals who would soon be Colonels again, and
Colonels who would soon be Majors. To have been,
through long uneventful unmental years, a peace-
time soldier puts the imagination in jeopardy and
is · apt to breed a self-centred fatuity, which the
inexperienced may easily mistake for deliberate
naughtiness. Yet these brave men, who hate peace
and despise civilians, have many human qualities.
They are generally polite to women, and they are
kind to animals and to those of their inferiors who
show them proper deference and salute them briskly.
It is not always easy to judge them fairly. And that
night one did not try. They jarred intolerably.
They seemed a portent, though in truth they were
something less. They found themselves left alone
to their private griefs, ruminating regretfully over the
golden age that had suddenly ended, gazing into the
blackness of a future without hope.

CHAPTER XLI

IN THE EUGANEAN HILLS

November 12th, 1918

I T is all over. For a few days it seemed possible
that we might be sent northward, through re-
deemed Trento and over the Brenner and the
crest of the Alps and down through Innsbruck, to open
a new front against Germany along the frontier of
Bavaria. But that will not be necessary now. It
is all over.

Our Battery is living partly in a little terra-cotta
Villa and partly in a barn close by. We are among
the Euganean Hills, a group of little humps, shaped
like sugar loaves, which rise out of the dead level
of the Venetian Plain, south-west of Padua. Here
Shelley wrote a famous and beautiful poem, and
Venice, on a clear day, is visible in the distance from
a monastery perched among trees upon one of the
loftiest humps. Our guns, which will never fire any
more, sit in a neat row, " dressed by the right," along
the garden path outside the Villa, their noses pointing
across a grass lawn. Their names, which are the
Battery's Italian history, are painted on their muzzles
and their trails in large white letters, picked out with
red upon a dark green ground : *Carso, Piave, Altipiano*
and *Trentino*. *Trentino* is my gun. They look very
ornamental in their new coats of paint, and with a
high polish on their unpainted metal parts.

It is an hour of anticlimax. There is nothing to
do, and one has to " make work " in a hundred silly,

ingenious ways. Next week some of the men who
have been out of England for 19 months will go
on leave. Then, after a fortnight in England, unless
something tremendous and unexpected happens, they
will all come back again. And there will still be
nothing to do. Was it Wordsworth who said that
poetry is " emotion remembered in tranquillity " ?
Wordsworth would undoubtedly have written much
poetry here. Our chief delight is Leary's musical
voice. He sings to us in the evenings after dinner,
" La Campana di San Giusto " and " Addio, mia bell',
addio " and choice stornelli, and " Come to Ferrara
with me," a cheerful song of his own composing, set
to a music-hall tune which was famous three years
ago, and " We'll all go a-hunting to-day,"-an old song
with a superb chorus. And so the days pass, one
very like another.

I dreamed last night that a regular soldier of high
degree and uncertain nationality appeared to me and
said, " Do you not see now, young man, that peace
is degeneracy, and that war is 'an ennobling discipline ? " And I, chancing my luck, replied, " Yes,
the great von Moltke himself said that peace is a
dream, and not even a beautiful dream." Whereupon
my visitor changed into a white owl and vanished
with a hoot. And I awoke, and found that I had
overslept myself and that the nine o'clock parade,
which I was due to attend, was already falling in
outside.

Then said I to myself bitterly, " At any rate we
here have all survived, and, therefore, since war is
the greatest of all biological tests, we must all be very
fit to have survived, especially that most fit young

man, who came out to the Battery from England a
day or two before the armistice was signed, after three
years at Shoeburyness, and the fittest of all must be
those whose survival, apart from such dangers as
influenza and air raids, has never been in doubt, the
valuable people who have been kept in England,
because they were members of concert parties or foot-
ball teams at the depôts, or officers' servants to influential *imboscati*, or influential *imboscati* themselves."

And then, with a great and well-disciplined effort,
I pulled my thoughts together, and said to myself,
" Enough of these musings of the peace-time soldier ! "

CHAPTER XLII

LAST THOUGHTS ON LEAVING ITALY

ON the 3rd of December I passed out of Italy,
after eighteen months spent as a soldier
within her borders.   These eighteen months
will always be lit up for me by the memory of a great
comradeship between men of Allied nations.   We have
lived together through the dark days and the sunshine,
through sorrow and joy, through uncertainty and
defeat to final victory.

I have been very fortunate in my personal relations
in Italy.   I have found always among Italians, both
civilian and military, and from simple soldier to
General, the most open friendliness, the most un-
sparing kindliness, the most happy spirit of good
fellowship.   And on my journey home I closed my
eyes and imagined myself back once more at Venice

in full Summer, and at Milan, and at hospitable
Ferrara, and at Rome in the Spring, and on the shores
of the Bay of Naples, and out on Capri, and in the
wonder world of Sicily,—and always among friends.
And then my steps went back in fancy to the battlefields, where our guns had been in action. I saw
again the great peaks and the precipitous valleys
of the Trentino. I saw the wreck of liberated Asiago,
ringed round with mountains whose sides were clothed
with shattered pine trees, heavy with snow, and I
went down once more by that astounding mountain
road from Granezza to Marostica, with the Venetian
Plain and all its cities spread out beneath my feet,
and Venice herself on the far horizon, amid the shimmer
of sunshine on the distant sea. I stood again on the
bridge at Bassano, looking up the Val Brenta, with
Monte Grappa towering above me on my right hand,
and then turning south-eastward across the level plain
I heard again the rushing waters of the Piave and,
crossing to the farther side, passed through Conegliano,
burnt out and ravaged, and Vittorio Veneto, a name
that will resound for ever, to the broken bridge over
the Meduna, east of Pordenone, and the village of
Nogaredo, whither I came as one of its first liberators.
And, as in a dream, I saw Udine, unspoilt and radiant
as she was fifteen months ago, before Caporetto,
and poor little Palmanova, as I last saw her, wreathed
in the black smoke of her own burning, and the
cypresses and the great church of Aquileia and the
lagoons of Grado.

Then the flying feet of memory carried me beyond
the Isonzo, up the wooded slopes of San Michele,
where the dead lie thicker, and along the Vippacco,

running swiftly between banks thick with acacias, and among the ruined suburbs of Gorizia, up towards those desolate lands, which for future generations of Italians will be, I think, the holiest ground of all,— the bare summit of Monte Santo, and the mountain-locked tableland of Bainsizza, and the rocky, inexorable Carso. These rocks have, perhaps, been more deeply soaked with blood than any other part of the entire Allied line on any continent. Here died many thousands of the bravest and the best of the youth of Italy. " Nella primavera si combatte e si muore, o soldato." How many great lovers, fathers, thinkers, poets, statesmen, that might have been, but never were, lie here ! These lands will ever be more thickly peopled with the cemeteries of the dead than with the villages of the living, lands desolate and barren, yet strange and beautiful. Clear and clean is the beauty of those graves in the noonday brightness, delicate and tremulous in the early dawn and in the soft light of a fading day, and for us, who think of those dead with a proud and tender emotion, that beauty is, in some sort, a frail consolation. The dust of strong men from the great mountains is buried here, and of men from the historic cities and the small unknown towns and the little white villages of Italy, and of peasants from the wide plains, and of brave men from the islands, and a handful of Frenchmen and Englishmen along with them, and very many of those tragic soldiers, drawn from many races, who died in the service of the Austro-Hungarian State, fighting against their own freedom. I see again, as vividly as though it were yesterday, those high-hearted legions of Italy, sturdy men and fresh-faced boys, going

forward with a frenzied courage, supported by an
Artillery preparation which elsewhere would have been
thought utterly insignificant, to assault positions which
elsewhere would have been declared impregnable.

" The world," said Lincoln at Gettysburg, " will
little note nor long remember what we say here, but
it can never forget what they did here. It is for us,
the living, rather to be dedicated here to the unfinished work which they who fought here have thus
far so nobly advanced ; that from these honoured
dead we take increased devotion to that cause for
which they gave the last full measure of devotion ;
that we here highly resolve that these dead shall not
have died in vain." So may it be ! They died for
the dream of a greater, a free and a secure Italy, and,
the more reflective of them, for a better, more coherent
world and no more war. A part of their dream is
already come true, but part is a dream still, a debt
to them that only we can pay. It will need to be a
far better world, with a progress sustained and ever
growing through centuries to come, if this tremendous
sum of wasted youth, of broken hearts, of embittered
souls, of moral degradation, of wounds that cannot
be healed until all this ill-fated generation has passed
away, if this great sum of past and present evil is to
be cancelled by future good in the cold balance of
historic reality. Of the dead we may say, their task
is over, their warfare is accomplished. But not of
the living. The future is theirs, to make or mar.